INDIAN SOCIALISM

About the Author

Prof. V.K.R.V. RAO (*b.* 1903) had his economic training in Bombay and Cambridge. He joined the University of Delhi as its first Professor in 1942 and subsequently became its Vice-Chancellor. He has received many honours, including the D.C.L. (Honoris Causa) of Oxford University and the Padma Vibhushan from the President of India. He has served on several national and international committees, and functioned as Honorary Chairman of the United Nations Sub-Commission on Economic Development from 1947 to 1950. He has a large number of publications to his credit, including one on Swami Vivekananda as the Prophet of Vedantic Socialism. He has also been a Member of the Planning Commission of India from 1963 to 1966 and Cabinet Minister of the Indian Government from 1967 to 1971.

From his college days, in the company of Yusuf Meherally, to this day when he is living in retirement in Bangalore and devoting himself to academic writing, Dr Rao has been a Democratic Socialist.

He has spoken on many platforms and written many articles on his democratic socialist faith, which gained in later years by the growing impact of the gandhian approach on his thinking. While he never participated in active party politics, he was always taking part in public affairs, mainly on economic or egalitarian issues. This volume on Indian Socialism is his first publication in book from of his life-long interest in Democratic socialism.

INDIAN SOCIALISM

Retrospect and Prospect

V.K.R.V. RAO

CONCEPT PUBLISHING COMPANY PVT. LTD.
NEW DELHI-110059

ISBN: 978-81-7022-161-6

Edition 2025

Published and Printed by

Concept Since 1974

Concept Publishing Company Pvt. Ltd.
A/15-16, Commercial Block, Mohan Garden,
New Delhi-110059 (India)
T: 91-11-41101460
E: publishing@conceptpub.com, *W*: www.conceptpub.com

Preface

IN SPITE of its comparative slimness, this volume has had a long gestation period. It may never have been sent for publication but for the insistence of a friend to whom I had mentioned it casually and who thereafter gave me no peace till I finished it. The title I had given to the original version was the "Indian Approach to Socialism". In its largely revised form and with its additional chapters, I have given it a new title, *Indian Socialism : Retrospect and Prospect*.

The book is divided into two parts. Part one is entitled "The Background to Indian Socialism" and has four chapters. The first deals with the non-Indian background, and the second with the capitalist and communist alternatives to economic development. The third chapter talks of the democratic socialist alternative to the capitalist and communist ways for achieving economic development without either political regimentation or economic inequality. The fourth chapter outlines the alternative presented by Gandhi for establishing what may be loosely described as a socialist society based on trusteeship and non-violence and with a minimum role given to government in its establishment or operation. Part two deals with the "Indian Socialist Experiment" and covers the remaining chapters 5 to 9 in the book. Chapter 5 deals with the Indian approach to socialism according to my understanding, while chapters 6 and 7 deal with the Indian socialist experiment with a mixed economy as its instrument; chapter 8 raises the rhetorical question "Did India Miss the Socialist Bus?", and deals with the politics of the Congress, Socialist and Communist parties in this context during the forties and early fifties. Chapter 9 brings the book to a close with my speculative observations on where we go from here and the possibility of reviving the task of taking India to a democratic socialist society.

I would be failing in my duty if I did not thank Prof Amal Ray and Prof M V Nadkarni of the Institute for Social and Economic Change, Bangalore and Prof Sukhamoy Chakravarthy of the Delhi School of Economics and Prof P C Joshi of the Institute of Economic Growth for going through this manuscript and giving me their comments and suggestions for improvement. I must add that while credit is due to them for such improvements as they stimulated, the entire responsibility is mine for all the errors of omission and commission in history, logic and understanding that this book may continue to retain.

If this book evokes some discussion and leads to some new thinking and a new striving for establishing a democratic socialist society in India, I shall feel amply rewarded for both my labour and my temerity in writing it.

Institute for Social and
Economic Change
BANGALORE
26 February 1982

V K R V RAO

Contents

PART ONE

THE BACKGROUND TO INDIAN SOCIALISM

The Non-Indian Background 1

WHILE the Indian approach to socialism has undoubted links with indigenous Indian thought and philosophic traditions, there can also be no doubt about the influence that western thinking and experience has had on its development. It may therefore be appropriate to begin this study with a brief account of the history of economic development in the west and the socialist ideas that emerged thereform. It would also be relevant to take a brief look at the unexpected turn that socialism took in finding implementation in the under-developed and under-industrialised eastern regions of the west (and later, in the east), rather than in the developed and industrialised nations of the western part of the west (or in the east) in spite of their large concentration of industrial workers and the appeal of the Marxist prognosis for their social evolution. It must be added that this chapter does not profess to be an original contribution. It only attempts a bird's eye view of the subject and is based on work done by scholars in the field of economic development and of socialist thought.

The industrial revolution brought in its wake vast opportunities for economic growth with its implicit possibilities of both betterment in mass welfare and deepening inequalities in income, wealth and economic power. The use of machinery and energy involved substantial capital accumulation. This was effected by exploitation of colonies and dependencies in Asia, Africa and Latin America, and of the domestic working classes, and mobilisation of a large part of the incremental output resulting from the new methods of production. The inhuman practices that accompanied the emergence and development of capitalism, especially in the United Kingdom, where it first took birth, shocked the conscience of sensitive citizens and led to a spate of ideas and movements for humanising the capitalist process of development. This was accompanied by simultaneous attempts at the establishment of a parliamentary democracy for transfer of political power to the masses and of trade union organisation that would give power to the working class. Exploitation of the national masses gradually gave way to colonial exploitation of foreign peoples. By the end of the nineteenth century, capitalism had matured in the United Kingdom and was in fact trying to develop some benevolent features for its domestic workers. Meanwhile, the capitalist system had also developed in other western countries; and the twentieth century was initiated by competition among the developed capitalist countries. Capitalism combined with competitive imperialism; the outcome was the first World War of 1914-19 which led to the emergence on the international scene of new capitalist powers, namely the United States of America and Japan. The inter-war period saw the development of the United States as the major capitalist power, the decline of the Western European capitalist powers like Great Britain and France, the growth of Japan as an imperialist power, the emergence of Italy as a fascist country and the fantastic development of Germany as a strong, well equipped and powerful Nazi nation attaining respectability as the bastion of anti-communism. The same period saw the birth and development of the Soviet Union as the first communist state in a hostile capitalist and fascist world and rallying point for communist forces and parties all over the globe; simultaneously, the forces of democratic socialism were growing in some of the capitalist democracies of the western world. The capitalist powers clashed again, but this time an anti-capitalist state like the Soviet Union was a participant on one side, and the result was World War II from 1939 to 1945. The aftermath of the second World War was a maze of contradictory developments; the Soviet Union and the United States emerging as the two major world powers, Germany and Japan recovering and attaining startling growth as capitalist economies, communism spreading over all the countries of eastern Europe, and China emerging as a major communist power in Asia. Capitalism has neither died nor has it attained world hegemony. Communism has grown but only as national governments, and has also failed to achieve world hegemony. The colonial world has attained political freedom, but with the exception of India and a few other countries, most of them have neither gone in for parliamentary democracy nor for communist rule but constitute a strange mixture of regimentation, capitalism and leftist professions if not practices. The cold war has given way to detente diplomacy, communist theories and practices are undergoing change, and so are capitalist theories and practices. And the world is a curious medley of ideological confusion, power politics, nationalist conflicts, threats of environmental pollution and depleting resources, and western intellectuals attacking poverty and preaching revolution in the erstwhile colonial world, while expressing disillusionment with their affluence at home. Now there is a widening belief in the limits of economic growth and disbelief in the unqualified benefits from large enterprises, a nostalgic regard for the small man and the still attractive countryside, and some talk of the relevance of Gandhian ideas on economic development. All this has naturally had its influence on the evolution of the Indian approach to socialism.

Before proceeding to outline the growth of the Indian approach to socialism, it would be appropriate to ask certain crucial questions regarding societal evolution that arise from the history of the last 150 years, as these have also a bearing on the Indian problem. These questions are :

1. Why did the Marxist prognosis of economic development fail in the mature capitalist economies of the western world?
2. Why did the first communist state emerge in an underdeveloped, feudal and largely agrarian nation?
3. What is the riddle behind the new communist state of China and its non-classical strategy for economic development?
4. Why are there divisions among the communist powers even as there are among the capitalist ones?
5. How far are existing capitalist societies true to capitalist ideology, and how far are existing communist societies true to theirs?

6. Why is there a growing acceptance of co-existence between capitalist and communist systems and a dimming of the vision for a global socialist order?
7. Is the world going in for a compromise system between capitalist and communist societies? Or are the two systems converging towards one another and evolving into a new system with its own distinctive identity?

These questions shall be dealt with seriatim but in summary fashion.

I. The Marxist prognosis failed to work in the developed capitalist economies because of the following reasons.

1. The clientele on whose discontent and subsequent action the Marxist prognosis is based is the proletariat constituted by the industrial workers and poor peasants. While the capitalist economies of the west did have such a proletariat in the earliest stages of their development, the position soon changed because of their acquisition and colonial exploitation of countries with rich natural resources and their continued domination of the world economy. These gains from colonial exploitation were shared by them, with the industrial working class and the poor peasantry who now got industrial employment. The result was that what might have been a revolutionary ardour leading to total change was replaced by reformist zeal content with modifications in the capitalist system; and the Marxist prognosis failed to click.
2. The capitalist classes, for varied reasons, were not able to keep wages down at subsistence level nor did the labour force population multiply on Malthusian assumptions and help to keep wages at subsistence levels. In fact, while profits increased and the capitalist classes became more affluent, there was also a steady rise in the level of real wages over the decades.
3. The rise of the middle class in both numbers and influence led to the spread of liberal values and

helped to build up parliamentary democracy and with it the dilution of the coercive power of the state to function solely as a guardian of capitalist interests and owners of private property in means of production.

4. Parliamentary democracy, liberal values, and concentration of industrial workers helped the working classes to organise themselves; and trade unions were able to use collective bargaining to better the earnings and working conditions of the industrial labour force and minimise their exploitation by the capitalist classes.
5. The crisis of mass unemployment faced by the capitalist countries on account of trade-cycles and slumps was successfully tackled to a large extent by the application of Keynesian techniques and did not therefore result in a revolutionary situation.
6. Nationalism generated during the course of World Wars I and II had its effect on the working classes in the capitalist countries. The bourgeois sentiments created in these countries with their anti-communist slant also had their effect on these working classes. Even the current inflationary crisis enveloping the capitalist world, while causing industrial troubles, had not led the working class to agitate for the establishment of a workers' state in their countries nor plan for a civil war to capture class-based political control over the state apparatus.

If captialism does eventually collapse—and this appears very unlikely—in these countries, it would be for reasons different from those outlined in the Marxist prognosis, and no forecast can be made with any confidence about what form its replacement would take.

II. As regards the second question as to why contrary to the Marxist prognosis, a communist state emerged in a feudal, agrarian and under-industrialised society like czarist Russia, no logical answer has yet been found which can be considered satisfactory. There is no doubt that the lack of popular support for the czarist regime, the appalling defeat of the Russian armed forces in World War I, and German readiness to let in Lenin and his comrades into Russian territory, all did play a part in facilitating the October Revolution. So did the communist underground which had been built up over years of czarist oppression among the soldiers and industrial workers of Russia. Nor could there be any doubt about the great personal role played by Lenin through his long years of intellectual contributions on communism, his building up of a dedicated team of party workers and above all the superb generalship he displayed through changing situations to install the Bolshevik Party in power over the state apparatus. This he could do because though the overthrow of the czarist government was accomplished by the middle class liberal party of the Mensheviks, they could not maintain law and order against the still powerful reactionary feudal forces nor the newly militant working classes and disbanded rank and file of the armed forces. The inane and futile bid by the victorious capitalist nations of World War I to intervene in Russia and prevent the emergence of communist power also played an unintended role in strengthening Lenin and the success of the October Revolution. But from a purely objective point of view, it was the effectiveness and weakness of the liberal middle classes who controlled the provisional government that made for the crumbling of Russian state power at the first massive and opportune onslaught by the working class. There can also be no doubt that it was the absence of capitalist development on the scale necessary for strengthening and dynamising of the coercive state apparatus and its establishment of a powerful middle class wedded to and believing in the captialist system that made the Russian state so vulnerable to the communist attack. It almost appears that it is inadequate capitalist development and surviving feudalism rather than abolition of feudalism and its replacement by mature capitalism that created the conditions for a successful revolutionary take-over of the state by the working class. But one would not venture of commit oneself to such a generalisation without a deeper study. But what would be acceptable is the catalytic role played by Lenin's revolutionary genius in harnessing the support of the vast and deprived masses of the country to the precarious hold his working class had secured on the Russian state. Thus the landlords were liquidated, land was redistributed among the land-hungry and landless peasantry of the country, the workers were permitted temporarily to take complete control over their factories and feel important, and the soldiers were satisfied with the introduction of democratic procedures and the establishment of an easy camaraderie with their officers. Lenin had embarked on instituting a proletarian dictatorship in place of the liberal democracy that the Mensheviks had been trying to install. This was followed by Lenin's famous programme of literacy plus electricity, the opening of undreamt of opportunities to the sons and daughters of the poor and the deprived, continuous education of the workers in communist principles, and the building up of a strong and committed cadre of party workers who were posted in every important place of production, and collective functioning of peasants, workers and government officials. The party was placed in command and provided integration and unity of purpose to the working of both the administration and economy of the country. Five year plans were formulated and economic development given high priority with emphasis on heavy industries, capital accumulation and enforcement of austere standards of consumption on the entire population including party cadres, government officials and the leadership. The Soviet Union developed as the world's first socialist economy and successfully withstood the Hitlerite invasion. And today it is one of the two big powers in the world, the other one being the United States of America with its opposing ideology. The Revolution came to Russia partly as a result of the accidents of war, partly from the long preparatory work of building underground forces of dissent, partly from the almost inherent weakness shown by the liberal democratic forces and above all, from the splendid strategy and superb leadership shown by Lenin. The Revolution succeeded because there was neither a strong capitalist state nor a solid middle class to oppose it. It could consolidate itself and establish a viable socialist state because of the way its leadership, in spite of its comparatively small numerical following, was able to harness the support of the masses by its physical liquidation of landlords, feudal chiefs and other oppressors, and giving the masses a vested interest in the new system by the redistribution of property and an opportunity for a new and self-respecting life. It then assumed stability and achieved by one-party rule, a strongly regimented state in the political field and development in the economic field through a socialist planning.

The Marxian prognosis has been fulfilled to the extent that a proletarian dictatorship was established, but not in the context of a mature capitalism as anticipated in that prognosis.

III. As regards the Chinese communist state, that again has not followed the classic Marxist prescription. China was also a largely agrarian and under-industrialised economy and its ruling class led by Chiang Kai Shek was also feudal in character and corrupt in its administration when Mao was able to take over power in 1949. Chiang Kai Shek's forces had also been defeated during the second World War as the Russian forces were during the first World War; and his eventual victory was solely the gift of the Allied Powers and did not ensure the public support that may have come if he had been able to fight the Japanese successfully on his own. The power of the state that he controlled was largely that of a paper tiger while Mao on the other hand had a dedicated team of Communist party workers and in addition a disciplined Chinese Communist army of his own which could now overwhelm the demoralised and unicommitted forces of Chiang Kai Shek. There again there was no solid middle class wedded to capitalism to oppose the communists as the country was still economically backward and industrially underdeveloped. And like Lenin in Russia, Mao also provided effective strategy and superb leadership in the capture of state power. So far, the Chinese experience was to a considerable extent on par with the Russian experience and, like it, was far from being an illustration of the viability of the Marxist prognosis. The Chinese riddle however lay in the stress that Mao and his colleagues laid on the peasant, agriculture and rural development, and not on just the leadership of the working class and the development of heavy industry that had accompanied the Russian experiment. Mobilisation of labour rather than capital accumulation, and belief in the revolutionary role of the peasantry rather than its denigration in favour of the industrial working class constituted the major difference in the development process between Chinese and Soviet communism. And yet, Chinese communism proved to be as stable and self-sustaining as Soviet communism and today communist China also ranks as a major world power, though not on par with the Soviet Union. However, it is not clear how long China will continue in this path now that Mao has left the scene, nor whether and how soon she would revert to the Soviet style of economic development, which she had adopted during the earliei years of her communist regime.

Since this was written, it appears that China is now going in for a revised economic policy with a new emphasis on the use of modern science and technology, import of foreign capital and equipment, more stress on larger production units and a technology of development more in common with that of the western countries and the Soviet Union than had been the case after the cultural revolution, the great leap forward and Mao's ideologically determined economic programme. All the same, there is no doubt that the emphasis laid in the communist developmental process in China on labour mobilisation, small production units, rural communes, production brigades, agricultural development, and decentralisation of economic activity with regional and local self-reliance are having a profound impact on socialist thinking in the populous countries of the developing world and giving added strength to the similar ideas current in the Indian approach to socialism.

IV. Divisions that are now more than apparent among states styling themselves as communist, constitute a sad commentary on the ringing call to the workers of the world to unite 'as they have nothing to shake off except their chains' which constituted the peroration of the Communist Manifesto of 1848 drafted by Marx himself. There have always been differences between working class organisations in the capitalist countries and now we see differences between working class opinion among the communist countries themselves. It is true that there have always been differences and factions within the Communist parties both at the national and international level; but during the earlier years they were based mainly on ideological grounds. At the national level, differences appear to be based more on power politics and factions, though there may also be some ideological overtones relating to the position of the individual. At the international level, differences have mainly been based on divergence in national interests, its most conspicuous illustration being found in the cold war that has been in progress during the last few years between China and the Soviet Union. Initially, perhaps it was a case of country like China with its long cultural history resenting the arrogant claim of leadership of the communist world proclaimed by the Soviet Union which was a comparative newcomer in the cultural field, followed by China's desire at least to have leadership of Asian Communist parties as an Asian nation. As it developed however it became more firmly based on divergence of national interests. International differences have also begun to exhibit themselves between Communist parties in countries where they are not in power as in France and Italy and where they are as in the Soviet Union and some of its East European allies. These differences rest both on a consideration of national expediency for the capture of power through the democratic process and an ideological revision of some of the basic tenets of Marxist communism. Ideological revisionism seems also to be creating difficulties even within the countries under communist governments, not only in Eastern Europe but even within the Soviet Union. On the whole, the process appears somewhat similar to what had happened to old world Christendom and old world Islam, with trans-national dominion giving way to national autonomy and adjustments to individual national circumstances. Thus communism is taking national orientations and deviations and ceasing to be the world force which once could evoke loyalty transcending national barriers. To the extent that communism is now coming to terms with nationalism, the chances of the reorientation of capitalist societies and the developing countries in a communist direction have improved, though it will still have to contend with the vested interests of private property and private profit where these are wedded to a solid middle class in the country concerned. Paradoxically therefore the chance of a reorientation of non-communist countries in a communist direction have increased with the breakdown of a monolithic global communist vision with its centre in Moscow.

V. It is apparent that existing capitalist societies are no longer functioning in conformity to capitalist ideology, especially on its economic side. Thus, free competition is only a textbook maxim, free enterprise is largely dependent on governmental support, direction and regulation, and the public sector is playing an increasing role in all sectors of economic activity in the so-called capitalist societies of the west. Market forces are diluted by advertisement, protectionism, subsidies, governmental patronage and military requirements. What survives in the contemporary capitalist world is private property in many of the means of production, the major role of the profit motive in economic decision making in the private sector, inequalities in private incomes, consumption and wealth, capitalist influence on political behaviour and power, and a solid middle class which now includes a significant section of the working class with a strong bourgeois culture and a firmly held anti-communist ideology. Capitalism today is more a negative platform of anti-statism and anti-egalitarianism than a positive one of free enterprise, free competition and the invisible hand harmonising private profit with public interest. The recent outpourings of Reaganomics is only a passing phase, more words and noise than actual action, and cannot set back the clock of capitalist evolution from competitive individual free enterprise, disdainful of state aid, to the monopolistic, oligopolistic and capital oriented corporate enterprise heavily dependent on state aid and using political influence and governmental regulations and policies as crutches for survival, if not also expansion. Even within the four years of his presidency, Mr Reagan may have to change his mission; and very definitely his successor is bound to do so. Capitalist evolution in the direction of state dependence, and welfare statism and people's democracy has come to stay; and it is this which makes for its possible convergence with non-capitalist or outer-capitalist societies whose economics and politics seem to be approaching the same road, though from a different direction.

As regards communist societies also, deviations have developed from their original ideological foundations. While traditional class inequalities have disappeared, vast opportunities for betterment given to the members of the previously suppressed and deprived sections of the population, and means of production are all owned by the state, inequalities of income and levels of living have reappeared; the party cadres and the bureaucracy, both of which are interlinked, have become the powerful ruling class against whom neither the common man nor the voice of dissent has but little chance; and the working class does not have the individual freedom associated with parliamentary democracy on the plea that the state itself is under their control. Market forces and the profit motive have been brought back though under state control and regulations. The major accent of the state and the party is still on capital accumulation and heavy industry, power still continues to be centralised, civil and intellectual freedoms are subject to a restraint that is not found in capitalist democracies, and foreign policy is attuned to national interests rather than to working class solidarity cutting across national frontiers. A new class has emerged in communist societies and it seems to be developing its own technique for survival, while its control over the state apparatus is more complete than what the capitalist classes have over their state machinery. The idyllic society envisaged by Marx as the end product of the revolution is still far off, the so-called proletarian dictatorship which really means a one party rule still continues, the state is becoming more powerful rather than showing any signs of weakening, let alone withering away, and one does not see the end of the so-called socialist transition nor do the forces fostered under the transition show any tendency to move in the direction of the Marxist societal ideal. While the communist states have all the paraphernalia of legislative democracy, and socialist economy, they have not been able to establish either a socialist ethic or a socialist psychology or an increased competitive efficiency which alone can ensure its long term internal survival, quite apart from its substituting itself for the capitalist system now operating elsewhere. In the actual working of its economy, the communist state is beginning to get nearer to the working of the capitalist economy with its giant corporations and professional management and the professional sharing power with the politician, except that the checks and balances found in the power structure of capitalist societies are not found in equal measure among the communist societies. On the whole, recent history has shown that both capitalism and communism have travelled a long way from the philosophy and ideology that either gave them birth or were put forward in justification of their maintenance. And in the process, they seem to be showing more similarities than differences as far as the working of their economies is concerned, as also in regard to the priority that national interests command over their political behaviour.

VI. The dimming of the vision for a global socialist order envisaged by the so-called scientific socialism or Marxian communism is the natural outcome of the developments we have indicated earlier in the actual working of the mature capitalist economies and of the several decades of working of the socialist societies which are still professedly in the transitional stage towards communism. The need for survival is mellowing the capitalist society which in turn is weakening the revolutionary fervour for a socialist change, while the harsh and untameable facts of human nature seen in the working of socialist economies is furthering the weakening process. The succession of Lenin by Stalin, Kruschev and Brezhnev and the policies followed by the Soviet Union both at home and abroad have not added to the enthusiasm of the intellectual socialist idealogue. And the enthusiasm with which Mao's attempt at preserving socialist integrity and changing human nature was greeted by socialist intellectuals has now started giving way to disillusion stemming from the Chinese aftermath following the death of Mao. And the disillusion has deepened with the realisation of the sway of nationalism over communism in the socialist operating countries and the use that it has made of nationalism elsewhere against the very interests of the proletariat whom it should have befriended. The role that the Soviet Union and China have played in recent years, whether in Asia or in Africa or in the Middle East, has not helped to maintain the credibility of their socialist ideology nor has the cold war that they are waging against each other. The socialist intellectual is finding that ranged against socialism are not only the vested interests of the capitalist classes and the state power they command but also nationalism, racism, traditional beliefs, and even linguism, and above all, the stubborn facts of human nature which seem impervious either to the lure or to the coercion of both socialist philosophy and the power of the socialist state. Nor can he get satisfaction from the increase in the number of states that call themselves socialist, as they seem to be as much in the game of power politics for national advancement as the capitalist powers. It is therefore not surprising that the intellectual's vision of a global socialist society has now become dim. It is in fact to his credit that he still continues to be swayed by the ideology of socialist change, at least in his own country. Here of course the reference is not to those intellectuals who live with capitalism at home and enjoy its fruits but would like to foster socialism abroad.

This dimming of a world socialist vision has led to a certain loosening of the tensions between the capitalist and communist state powers in the world. The capitalist powers are no longer terrified by the thought of a world communist bogey and have learnt that the communist world also has its divisions which can be exploited. Likewise, the communist powers are no longer afraid of wars of capitalist intervention and have found that the capitalist powers have their national differences which the communist powers can also exploit to their own advantage. Diplomacy has now taken over; and though the battle continues in conference rooms and in chanceries, there is no real threat of armed conflict between capitalist powers and communist powers on ideological grounds. The real reason behind the acceptance of co-existence between them however is the sharing of nuclear power between them and the virtual impossiblity of using it because of the threat it holds of mutual destruction and indeed the destruction of the rest of the world as well. It is this nuclear balance and the military stalemate it has brought between the U.S.A. and the U.S.S.R. that is the basic material reason behind the detente and the development of the doctrine of co-existence. The two systems, however, can still compete on the international stage for establishing their influence, if not their ideology, on the vast number of uncommitted nations of the Third World which possess such a large share of the world's non-renewable resources of energy and strategic minerals. This they do by propaganda, education, economic and military aid, diplomacy and advertisement of the relative efficiency of their economic, scientific and technological achievements. The war of ideological propaganda goes on, intervention by subversion and corruption has been substituted for force and threat of force, socialist minded intellectuals from the west are foot-lose in the Third World along with their capitalist counterparts, and there is a great deal of din and ideological noise. But everyone knows that behind it all is a great deal of play acting, the real motivation is power politics and national interests of both the capitalist and the communist powers, and there is no prospect of any establishment of a global socialist order as was dreamt of by the radicals of the later half of the 19th and the earlier half of the 20th centuries.

VII. Does this detente, coexistence, and military stalemate and decreasing divergence in economic techniques used by the capitalist and communist powers mean that the two systems are converging towards one another and the world is on the way to evolving a compromise system that will eventually take place of both as a global societal order? The answer would be an emphatic negative. This is not only because of the posture of aggressive confrontation that the United States is now adopting towards the Soviet Union and its attempt to encircle it by its arming of Pakistan, its growing military presence in the Indian Ocean, and its new concord with China, and the obstinacy of the Soviet Union in retaining large military forces in Afghanistan, and the sudden infusion of heat into the cold war. It is also, and in secular terms much more strongly based on the fact that the basic difference between the two systems in terms of ownership of private property in the means of production, and the dependence of employment on private capital will still continue; and as long as it does, there can be no possibility of their converging into one compromise system. Nor can one ignore the new form that aggressive capitalism is taking, with giant multinational corporations taking global strides over the world and becoming a law unto themselves. Nobody seems to be in a position to control or even regulate their activities. What seems clear, however, is that behind their aggressive advance there is a distinct ideology and that is the ideology of capitalism. One does not see how, in a world of growing multinational corporations, there can be any chance of the capitalist, the socialist and the uncommitted world getting together in a compromise system. Nor can one see any real possibility of either the capitalist or the socialist system giving up its different political processes for the acquisition of state power and control of the governmental machine of coercion and patronage. As far as the Third World is concerned, it needs economic development for solving its problem of poverty and unemployment. At the same time it also needs the dovetailing of economic growth with social justice, as without it growth by itself can neither abolish poverty nor eliminate unemployment. Many countries in the Third World have also inherited western liberal traditions in the political field and of civil liberty, and some of them have now made them their own. What effect all these will have on their ideological approach is a matter that only the future can tell. But as far as India is concerned, a socialist approach has almost become a national consensus, though its acceptability in practice will turn upon the extent to which it can solve the problems of growth and social justice, the abolition of poverty and the removal of unemployment, and the retention of the political values it has now enshrined as its own. While the precondition is economic growth, growth without social justice is unacceptable. What kind of a system will do this and at the same time be feasible within the constraints of parliamentary democracy and civil freedom is the problem that confronts the Indian approach to socialism.

Before outlining the influences that have developed the socialist approach of an Indian vintage, it may be useful to look at the way in which capitalist and communist powers have tackled the problem of economic growth, social justice and political values and the lessons it holds for us in India in attempting a socialist approach to the Indian economic problem.

2 The Capitalist and Communist Alternatives to Economic Development

FOR COUNTRIES of the Third World, which had been under colonial rule or influence for many decades, the most urgent problem posed by independence was economic development. Without economic growth, they could not solve their problems of poverty and unemployment nor improve their national levels of living. Historically, capitalism had proved its efficiency as an instrument for economic growth, while in recent decades, communism had also given a good account of itself in the same field. As ideology is a powerful motivating force in the developing countries and as they were also keen on economic growth, it would be relevant to consider here the two systems as alternative methods for economic development. It is particularly necessary to do so in the Indian context which is witnessing the emergence of an Indian approach to socialism.

Capitalist economies left to the individual or corporate entrepreneur the major role in economic development. The decisions which were taken regarding consumption and saving, the volume and pattern of investment, and the product-mix were all decisions taken by individuals or corporations. These decisions were taken in response to the stimuli offered by the market, which is a compound of decisions regarding purchases and sales taken by individuals and corporations. The means of production were owned by individuals or groups of individuals combined in partnerships or joint stock companies. It was this ownership with which was linked the power to take the major economic decisions, namely, what to produce, how to produce, and how much to produce; while it was the individual or corporate consumer or recipient of income, whether from labour or property or from both, who decided what to buy, how much to buy and how much to save. The decisions regarding production were thus linked with the ownership of the means of production. Decisions regarding consumption were linked with the ownership of income, whether accruing from labour or property or both. Those who own means of production or hire them were the persons who employed labour and it was they who took the economic decisions and determined the disposal of the economic surplus. Prices were given by the market and determined by the forces of supply and demand, which in turn were determined by the pattern of income distribution, the schedule of wants, the state or knowledge and technology, and the dynamism and decision-making of entrepreneurs. Maximisation of the difference between price and cost of production acted as the motive force, and profit became the determinant of allocation of resources. In brief, private property in the means of production, freedom of individual and corporate enterprise, consumer sovereignty and free play of market forces became the characteristics of a capitalist society, with the entrepreneur as the key figure who operates the system.

The communist system, on the other hand gave the community (operating through some person or groups of persons who function on behalf of the community) the authority to take the major economic decisions. There was no private property in the means of production nor was there any hiring of wage labour by private individuals for purposes of production. The division of income between consumption and surplus was determined by the community, and therefore also the decisions regarding the volume of investment, the pattern of investment, and the product-mix. There was no free market and prices were more the result of deliberate decision by the community rather than of the spontaneous play of the forces of demand and supply. Similarly, the pattern of income distribution was more the result of deliberate decision by the community rather than of market forces and property relations. Like the capitalist society, the communist society also had prices, incomes, wages and markets; but the forces determining them were different in the two societies. Thus in the communist society, the means of production are owned by the community, the community takes on the entrepreneurial function, consumer sovereignty is diluted by the economic decision-making of the community, and the market becomes an instrument for the implementation of the decision rather than a determinant of the volume and composition of the national product.

There are thus vast differences in the institutional framework and the social philosophy governing the working of the capitalist and communist systems of society. What difference does this make to the methods they follow in the process of economic development?

Economic development as such has certain features that are independent of the system under which it takes place. The operational part of development is the increasing of investment, the pattern given to the increased investment, the efficiency with which the additional investment yields an increased output of goods and services, the extent to which the increased income is saved and invested, the pattern given to the additional investment, and so on till the circle is completed and starts again. Accumulation of capital and betterment of human skills are both common to the capitalist and communist methods of economic development. The pain involved in the task of accumulation is common to both; and this is amply borne out by the history of development under both the systems. Under the capitalist system, the worker is denied that increment in consumption that he desires and the surplus gets channelled into investment *via* the entrepreneur who ideally himself restrains his own consumption (at least in the earlier stages of development); while under the communist system, the same thing happens except that the surplus gets channelled into investment *via* the state.[1] Non-voluntary participation by the working class in the process of capital accumulation is common to the earlier stages of development in both the capitalist and communist economies. In both, we find exploitation,* accumulation and similar increase in that element in national income, which corresponds to profit in the case of the capitalist countries and to public revenues whether by way of tax surplus or net receipts of public enterprise in the case of the communist

The word 'exploitation' is used in the sense of denial to the worker of the whole product of his labour. It is this exploitation that leads to the emergence of what Marx called 'surplus value'.

countries. Where peasants formed a major section of the community and agriculture contributed a major portion of the national income, as it normally did in the earlier stages of development, the process of capital accumulation also involved the exploitation of agricultural classes. It was thus exploitation of labour, both industrial and agricultural, together with the application of new methods of production that enabled the required expansion of the economic surplus and, with it, the capital accumulation necessary for the take-off from pre-development to development. We may not all recognise this basic similarity in the real costs of development in both the capitalist and communist societies, but that is partly the result of the normal human tendency to overlook and slur over things that happened in the distant past as in capitalist countries, while simultaneously being shocked and appalled by the identical phenomenon if it happens within one's living experience, as in communist countries.

In spite of these basic similarities, the two systems have followed different techniques in the process of development; and it is this difference that is of absorbing interest to the countries that have either just undertaken or are still to undertake the task of economic development.

To begin with, a communist society must have economic planning and, whether centralised or decentralised, it must be planning on a national scale and, in fundamentals, at the national level. This is the reason why so many people identify planning in common parlance with communism. There can be no doubt that one cannot have communism without planning. But this does not mean that one cannot have planning without communism. Even in a capitalist society, there is some economic planning in the sense of projections, targets and economic decisions taken in advance of events. Thus farmers have their plans, industrialists have their plans, and big corporations have their plans. There is a great deal of perspective planning even in a capitalist society. Only these plans are individual or sectional. The decisions that emerge in a capitalist society are largely the result of the inter-play of decisions taken by a large number of individuals and groups, even though these may be based on their own individual plans and are influenced by government policies that affect costs, prices and profits.

But there is no one central body taking the crucial economic decisions in a capitalist society. This is the vital difference between a capitalist and a communist society; not the absence of any kind of planning, but the absence of national planning in the former and its inevitable presence in the latter.

Moreover, the very fact that vital economic decisions are taken as a result of national planning gives them a greater measure of certainty in implementation than when they are the result of the interaction of a series of individual and group decisions even if these are based on some kind of economic planning. In a capitalist society, one individual's decision to save may be nullified by another's decision to dis-save; whereas in a communist society, this does not happen as the decision to save is taken by the community and not left to the individual. Similarly, one individual's decision to step up investment may be negativated by another individual outbidding him in the purchase of factors of production for increasing consumption. There is no certainty in a capitalist society that anticipated savings will equal investment nor is it likely that demands will equal supplies at expected prices. In a communist society, on the other hand, there is a certain measure of certainty in the savings-consumption ratio, the pattern of investment, and the product-mix, provided, of course, the planning is effective and not just a facade of wishful thinking. Thus national planning and a certain measure of certainty in the collective implementation of desired economic decisions pertinent to economic growth distinguish the technique of economic development in a communist society from that in a capitalist society.

The second major difference between a capitalist and a communist society—and in some ways following as a consequence of the first distinction—is the higher rate of capital accumulation in a communist society. This is due to two factors, namely, a higher rate of saving, and a pattern of investment more oriented towards accelerating capital accumulation. These two factors act and react on each other and result in turn in giving a communist society a higher and quicker rate of capital accumulation.

Let us take the rate of saving first. The source of saving in any society, whether capitalist or communist, is the economic surplus. It is the magnitude and disposal of the economic surplus that determine the rate of saving in any society. In a capitalist society, the magnitude of this surplus depends upon the rate of profits, the level of wages, and the property relations that determine the distribution of the proceeds of production. Historically speaking, these factors worked in favour of a high rate of saving in the earlier stages of capitalist development, and it was this factor which led Marx to attribute a progressive bias to early capitalism in the task of capital accumulation. But it must not be forgotten that earlier capitalist development coincided in point of time with an un-free society, when the worker and peasant possessed neither political power nor class organisation and it was therefore possible for exploitation to increase the surplus. Colonial exploitation was another factor that added to the surplus in the metropolitan capitalist countries. It is also a fact that, during this early phase of capitalist development, the capitalist was a man with a mission who used himself almost as harshly his workers and restrained his consumption in order to increase the economic surplus. Self-exploitation by the the capitalist, exploitation of workers and peasants with the help of the state which the masses did not control, colonial exploitation of foreign peoples and resources, and a production mechanism based on property relationships all helped the early capitalist society to achieve a high rate of saving.[2] What is true of early capitalist development in the nineteenth century is, however not true of early capitalist development in the later half of the twentieth century; and it is this latter period which is relevant for the discussion of methods of economic development to the underdeveloped countries of emerging Asia and Africa to day. In the modern age, where the capitalist system has reached maturity in many parts of the world with consequential changes in the behaviour pattern of the capitalist, the balance of political power, and the structure of property relations, early capitalist development in the underdeveloped countries suffers from handicaps in increasing the economic surplus which its counterpart did not suffer from during the nineteenth century when capitalism itself was a new force in the social and political horizon. A capitalist society in a contemporary underdeveloped country cannot exert the same pressure on worker and peasant income which it could in the underdeveloped countries in the nineteenth century; and the rate of exploitation, on which depends the size of the economic surplus, cannot be equal to what it was then. Moreover, the capitalist in the contemporary underdeveloped world is of a different brand from his earlier counterpart in the nineteenth century. He is no longer the man of austerity who treats himself harshly and restrains his own consumption in order to increase the economic surplus. When the capitalist comes from abroad in the form of private foreign capital from developed capitalist societies, he brings along with him the standard of life and the consumption pattern that certainly does not err on the side of austerity. And when he is a native and claims indigenous roots, he is subject to the demonstration effect exerted by his compeers abroad and foreign capitalists at home, and is therefore not interested in restraining his own consumption and playing that role in increasing the economic surplus that his counterparts did in capitalist societies in the nineteenth century. The result is that the capitalist system does not lead to a high rate of saving in the contemporary world of underdeveloped countries.[3] In a communist society, on the other hand, there is hardly any scope for utilising the economic surplus for increasing consumption, as peasant and worker organisations are not permitted to play that kind of role vis-à-vis their levels of earnings and consumption standards that they do in contemporary capitalist societies, whether in developed or underdeveloped countries. In a communist society, there is no rent or profit accruing to private individuals; and therefore the whole of the surplus becomes available for savings and investment. There is also no inroad on this surplus by pressure, either political or organisational, of the workers and peasants. Politically, the workers and peasants are led by the Commnist Party, which has the same sense of mission and plays the same role in regard to capital accumulation as the capitalist entrepreneurs did during the early phases of capitalist development in the now developed capitalist societies. Organisationally the workers and peasants are led by the same Communist party, whose emphasis all the time is on production and accumulation rather than on consumption and immediate inroads into the increased production for purposes of increasing consumption. The rate of saving in a communist society is therefore likely to be much higher than in a capitalist society in the contemporary underdeveloped world. Whether it is higher than that in the earlier capitalist phase of the contemporary developed capitalist countries is a subject on which not enough data is available for an objective assessment. In any case, it is irrelevant as far as the contemporary underdeveloped world is concerned, for their interest lies in the rate of saving and how it is likely to behave under the capitalist and communist methods *now* rather than in the past.

The second major factor responsible for a higher rate of capital accumulation in a communist society is the pattern of investment. One is not referring in this connection to the somewhat futile controversy that takes place in the contemporary underdeveloped countries about the public versus private sector. A good deal of public investment that is taking place in the case of a country like India, for example, is no more than the building up of economic and social overheads, the infrastructure without which economic development is not possible, whether on capitalist or communist or socialist or other lines. In both capitalist and communist societies, as well as other societies which operate what is called a mixed economy, government plays a crucial role in the building of the infrastructure which makes expansion of production profitable for private enterprise and possible for public enterprise. One should not therefore mix up governmental investment in infrastructure with the pattern of investment that is peculiar to a communist society as distinguished from a capitalist society. When one talks of the pattern of investment in a communist society as more oriented towards capital accumulation, it refers to investment as between production of consumption goods and production of producer goods, the latter in turn being classified as producer goods for consumption industries, and producer goods for producer industries. The theoretical basis for this can be traced to Marx and his famous classification of the departments of production; but its importance in contemporary thinking on the promotion of economic growth owes much more to Soviet experience and the pattern of investment they have adopted in the planned economic development of their country. In a communist society, the pattern of investment is deliberately planned by central decision; and its emphasis is on producer goods rather than on that of consumption goods; and in producer goods, the producer goods for making produce goods rather than on producer goods for making consumption goods. In operational terms, this means higher priority in terms of time to producer goods for producing producer goods over producer goods for producing consumption goods, and to producer goods for producing consumer goods over consumption goods. The emphasis is thus more on productivity than on production, more on growth than on current consumption. and more on the future than on the immediate present. The task accepted by the communist system is a high rate of economic growth and therefore the pattern of investment takes the form of a high proportion of capital goods or of capital accumulation in depth, which has built-in factors for the automatic increase of capital accumulation. To quote from a well known and distinguished authority on Soviet planning.[4]

> As the principal branch in the sphere of material production, industry plays a leading and transforming part in building up the material and technical basis of socialism and communism. The leading branch of industry, heavy industry, comprises the foundation of the socialist economy, the technical basis for the continuous and intensive growth of the productive forces.

This was the reason why the First Soviet Five Year Plan not only provided for an unprecedented rate of investment (between a quarter and a third of the national income) but also assigned to heavy industry about three quarters of the amount invested in industry as a whole.[5] Moreover, in actual operation the rate of investment in heavy industry was considerably increased over the original estimates, mainly at the expense of light industry. The growth rate of capital goods in industrial output was permitted to decline over the subsequent five year plans as can be seen from the following Table 1, but nevertheless it continued to have priority over consumption goods and still continues to be the sheet-anchor of Soviet planning.[6]

TABLE 1 : **Average annual growth rate of gross industrial output in Soviet Union**

Period	Percentage for industry as a whole	of which: Output of the means of production (Group A)	Output of articles of consumption (Group B)
First Five Year Plan (last quarter of 1928-32)	19.2	28.5	11.7
Second Five Year Plan (1933-37)	17.1	19.0	14.8
Three Pre-war years of the 3rd F.ve Year Plan (38-40)	13.2	15.3	10.1
Fourth Five Year Plan (1946-50)	13.6	12.8	15.7
Fifth Five Year Plan (1951-55)	13.2	13.8	12.0
Seventh Five year Plan (1959-65)	8.6	9.3	7.3

In the case of capitalist society, on the other hand, the emphasis during the earlier stages was more on consumption goods and producer goods for producing consumption goods than on producer goods for producing producer goods. The pattern of investment has been, in historical terms, rather more on capital accumulation in volume than in depth, more on horizontal than on vertical expansion; and, while reducing the strain caused by capital accumulation, it also led to a lower rate of economic growth. It is not possible to be dogmatic about the system of priorities followed in the pattern of investment in capitalist development, partly because we do not have enough data on the subject and partly because of difficulties of interpretation arising from the very nature of investment in a capitalist society which is the result of the interplay of many and uncoordinated individual decisions. But it would be correct to say that, by and large, the priorities in the initial stages of capitalist development have been more on consumption goods and producer goods that would lead to an immediate increase in consumption goods rather than on producer goods as such. This has been well illustrated by Hoffman's study of *The Growth of Industrial Economies*, where he has shown that the proportion of consumption goods in their industrial output was very high during the earlier stages of industrial development in a number of capitalist societies and gradually declined with the growing maturity of these economies. He sums up in the following Table the overall trend he found in industrial development by analysing the changes in the relationship between the net output of consumer goods and capital goods industries in a number of economically developed countries.[7]

TABLE 2 : **Net output of consumer and capital goods industries as a percentage to total net industrial output**

	State of Industrialisation (in percentages)		
	First	Second	Third
Consumer-goods industries	83	71	50
Capital-goods industries	18	29	50

In fact, the proportion of consumer goods in industrial output has declined to about 30 per cent in recent years in the major economically developed countries such as the United States, the United Kingdom, Germany, Belgium and Japan. Thus, there is no difference between the capitalist and the communist system in regard to the place occupied by capital goods industries in the economy; only the process has taken a much longer period of time in the capitalist countries, as earlier priorities were on consumption goods; while in the case of communist countries, the time taken has been shorter, as earlier priorities were given to capital goods and that, too, by deliberate and centralised decision.

The combined effect of extracting a larger investible surplus and following a pattern of investment that places more emphasis on producer goods industries during the initial developmental stages had thus led to a higher rate of capital accumulation in the Soviet Union; in turn to a higher annual rate of economic growth in the Soviet Union than in the capitalist economies. This is well illustrated in the following Table.[8]

TABLE 3 : **Annual rates of growth in industrial output, 1860-1958 (Compound)**

Period	UK	USA	Germany	France	Italy	Sweden	Japan	USSR
1860-80	2.4	4.3	2.7	2.4	—	—	—	—
1880-1900	1.7	4.5	5.3	2.4	4.5	8.1	—	6.4
1900-13	2.2	5.2	4.4	3.7	5.6	3.5	3.8	4.8
1913-25-29	0.3	3.7	0.3	1.4	2.6	1.6	7.5	1.1
1925-29-38	3.1	-0.9	3.5	-0.7	1.7	5.4	6.5	17.2
1938-1958	2.9	5.3	3.5	3.6	4.3	3.5	3.4	8.9

It would be wrong to conclude however that the technique adopted for economic growth by the communist system is necessarily to be preferred to that adopted by the capitalist system. It all depends on the time-span envisaged for the growth period before it becomes self-sustaining, and the limits of political and social tolerance to the intensity of accumulation and delay in increasing consumption during this period. It was not merely a compulsory high rate of saving and an investment pattern that gave priority to producer goods that enabled the Soviet Union to have a rate of growth during this period. It was also the communist control of the state and society and the denial of individual liberty that accompanied it which made possible the successful adoption of this technique. And even the Soviet Union has had to dilute this technique and go in for giving a larger share to consumption goods in spite of the tight control its system has over its people. In fact many of the capitalist countries are at a higher stage of industrial and technological development, though the gestation period they had to undergo before reaching the stage reached by the Soviet Union was much longer. What the communist system did was to speed up economic growth in an effort to make up for lost time and not secure any appreciable advantages in comparative levels of contemporary economic development.

There are however some major differences in the economic development of capitalist and communist countries. One such difference is in respect of the performance of agriculture in their national economies. The technical methods followed for the development of agriculture productivity and expansion of agricultural production have been the same in both communist and capitalist economies, namely, mechanisation and modernisation, increase in the size of operational units, use of tractors and other farm machinery, and increasing inputs of chemical fertilisers, pesticides, etc. But communist agriculture has not shown the same results in terms of productivity and output as communist manufacturing industries. Nor has it given the same results as agriculture in the capitalist economies. The numerous crises through which Soviet agriculture has passed beginning with the great Kulak liquidation and collectivisation started by Stalin, the changing role of the machine tractor stations, the continuing (and in a way gradually extending) existence of a private sector and a free market within the collective farms, the association between the rise of Krushchev and his image as the one person taking agriculture the most seriously among Soviet leaders and determined to solve its problem, the not so recent decrease on an increase in the prices of Soviet farm products and the attempt to improve the terms of trade between Soviet agriculture and Soviet industry and between the rural and urban sectors—all these furnish ample evidence of the uneasy bed that the communist system has provided to agriculture in the Soviet Union. The comparative failure of the communist system to solve the problem of agriculture has been demonstrated even more clearly by the changes that have taken place in Yugoslav and Polish agriculture with their virtual repudiation of the basic Stalinist concept of Soviet agriculture. A more recent addition to the testimony has come from Communist China which continues to have a formidable agricultural problem, in spite of its accent on the peasant and on rural communes. And all this has been in contrast with the experience of agriculture in the capitalist societies led by the United States, where the problem has been one of how to deal with increasing agricultural production and agricultural surpluses. This comparative failure of communist agriculture as compared not only to capitalist agriculture but also to communist industry cannot be explained away in terms of difference in scientific knowledge and technical skills. The explanation has therefore to be sought in the differences between the two systems in terms of ideology or outlook, and agrarian structure.

Viewed objectively, it does appear that communist ideology is not specially committed to the peasant community. It is true that the party is called a Workers' and Peasants' Party, but the industrial worker, the urban resident, occupied the pride of place. By and large, communist theories, practice and slogans are linked with the worker who is identified with the proletariat; but workers meant in practice primarily industrial workers rather than even the poor peasants. The latter were regarded as socially less advanced and ideologically not fit to assume leadership because of their continuing subjection to feudal ideas and complexes. In fact, one of the acknowledged tasks of the communist society was to bring about a transformation of the peasantry and make them approximate to the industrial working class in their psychology, discipline, and capacity for co-ordinated and collective action. Thus, in some sense, the peasant in communist society felt himself a second class citizen rather than one of the elect; and this must have had some connection with the comparative failure of agriculture in communist societies to keep pace with industry in productive efficiency. There has been some change in Communist China in this matter, but not enough to bring up Chinese agriculture to American capitalist standards.

More important than this psychological impact was that caused by the changes in agrarian structure which communism brought in its train. Communist theory repudiates private property in the means of production and this applied to land as well. Private peasant agriculture therefore was brought to an end, the Kulaks (or more well-to-do and efficient farmers who generally also employed hired labour to assist them in farm operations) were liquidated, and collective farms became the ruling form of the communist agrarian structure. There were two major difficulties that appeared in their operation and were, in fact, inherent in the new structure. One was the difficulty of linking the distribution of farm output sufficiently with individual contribution to production on the farm, with a consequential reduction in the individual incentive for maximisation of output. The other was the undeniably adverse effect that absence of private property in land had on the farmer's incentive for maximising his effort. This was practically the universal experience of collectivised agriculture, in both the older and the newer communist societies, and led to the abrogation of collective farming and the virtual restoration of private property in land in at least two of the communist countries, namely, Poland and Yugoslavia. Even when it continued—as in the case of the Soviet Union and some of the other East European communist societies and now in Communist China, the system was diluted by the introduction of a certain element of private agriculture in the collective farms and the opportunity given for the sale of its output on a legally recognised free market. In spite of that, difficulties continued to exist in the task of maximising farm output; and, communist agriculture has failed to keep pace in efficiency either with communist industry or capitalist agriculture (as in the United States) or even peasant agriculture (as in Japan). The thesis put forward here is that there is something about land and agriculture that gives private property a far more positive role in the stimulation of productive capacity than appears to be the case with machinery and manufacturing industries. This contention is supported not only by the experience of industry in the Soviet Union and other communist countries but even by the experience of capitalist economies in the field of industry. Thus, in capitalist economies, private property is far more actively associated with enterprise and decision-making in agriculture than in the case of industry, where shareholders in giant corporations like Imperial Chemicals or Imperial Tobacco or Unilever for example, play hardly any role in decision-making.

The second major difference between the communist and capitalist methods of economic development that shows the former at a disadvantage stems from its centralisation of decision-making in economic affairs and the consequent growth of a vast and powerful bureaucracy. While such centralisation is of undoubted help in the allocation of resources between investment and consumption, the pattern of investment, and the composition of the product-mix, there is also no denying the adverse effect it has on local initiative, utilisation of individual enterprise and capacity for risk-taking, and maximisation of individual economic effort in terms of both intensity and of quality. Under the capitalist system, with its competition, profit making and possibilities of unlimited individual reward, individuals with resources are stimulated to put in their best efforts in their own interest, Adam Smith's 'divine hand' presumably performing the task of reconciling the results of such individual enterprise with collective requirements. Administrative decrees and bureaucratic guidance, even if backed by a strongly organised party and ideological enthusiasm, are no adequate substitute for the direct involvement of the individual in his economic activity through his self-interest and his desire for recognition and emulation. The result of this bureaucratisation of economic organisation, and economic decision-making at the top getting translated into orders at the bottom, is not only a reduction in individual efficiency, but also the emergence of numerous imbalances in detail. It also leads to an attempt at implementation of decrees through evasion of regulations by different units at the expense of one another rather than by an increase in total resources by invention and improvisation. Communist administrators and party officials have been conscious of the built-in dangers of bureaucracy that centralised planning involves; and no item has figured more in communist discussions and internal criticism than the dangers of bureaucracy. In fact, over the years, communist economic administration has been evolving a system of norms of performance, incentives, piece-wages, socialist emulation, decentralisation and other measures aimed precisely at this defect and providing communist substitutes for the capitalist system of private enterprise, competition and the free market in its effect on the release of maximum deployment of individuals with resources. The cardinal principle of economic stimulation is inducement. As the popular saying goes, 'you can take a horse to the water trough but you can't force it to drink'. What is true of the horse is even more true of man, especially when the activity desired is not just consumption, but active production. However, communistically inclined a person may be, there is a limit beyond which he will not just do what he is told, even if it is by communist authority. Force, even when backed by idealism, fails beyond a point. Human beings have their own ways of resisting force under any system when it is used to evoke positive responses; and postive responses are an essential condition for economic growth. The carrot is stronger than the whip in developing the economy. And one can say that the outstanding trend in communist economic administration over the years has been the substitution of the whip by the carrot. Thus, for practically every economic activity, an attempt has been made to create a norm, exceeding which results in extra payment, thus providing an incentive for increasing the intensity and quality of output of effort by labour. It is also widely believed that the norm is usually kept a little low, so that almost every one gets a little extra payment for exceeding it and also gets the feeling that he is participating in the development of the economy. With all these changes, however, though they are tending to minimise the adverse effect on individual initiative and effort that accompanies nationalisation of economic decisions, it still remains true that the capitalist system has an edge over the communist system in the matter of work motivation and individual response.

One more difference between the capitalist and communist methods of economic development may be mentioned before concluding this discussion. A capitalist society is an open society in the sense that no restrictions are placed on the free entry of visitors, import of private capital is allowed, and citizens are free to travel abroad, whereas the communist society is a closed society and has been guarded by what has come to be known as the 'iron curtain'. It is not necessary to deal here with the political aspect of the iron curtain or its relevance to civil liberties. But the iron curtain has certain important economic implications of considerable relevance to a developing economy. Economic development under the communist system aims at a rate of saving and investment that is not only high but also higher than what the people would go in for if they had a free choice. It becomes easier to do this ,if the people are not physically aware of the various consumption goods that those in the developed capitalist countries are having. After all, basic consumption goods, essential for existence, form a comparatively small proportion of family budgets in western countries. Much of the consumption is of a non-basic character and it is this which accounts for a lower rate of savings in the developed capitalist countries as also the higher preference for investment in consumption goods. If therefore non-basic consumption goods are kept out of the people's sight, it becomes easier to raise the rate of saving without causing stresses and strains among the people and without using batons and machine guns for dealing with the same. This is what the iron curtain did for the communist countries and it certainly facilitated a larger mobilisation of domestic resources for purposes of planned investment. In the case of the non-communist developing economies, the iron curtain does not exist; and the field is left free for the demonstration effect of the higher level and larger variety of consumption goods that people in capitalist countries enjoy. Private foreign capital that comes in brings with it foreign capitalists and technicians with levels of consumption that have a big demonstration effect on the local elite and leaders. This effect is further reinforced by the experience of those citizens who go abroad and bring back with them a taste for and tales of non-basic consumption goods that they have seen during their foreign sojourn. The result is that the upper classes in the non-communist developing economies seek a higher level of consumption and therefore save less; and this, in turn, has a demonstration effect on the common masses in their countries and makes it more difficult to get them to accept austerity during the period of development. Thus, the iron curtain, irrespective of its other aspects with which it is so closely identified with a communist regime, helps it in having a higher rate of saving than its absence does in the open societies characteristic of capitalist regimes.

To sum up, the communist system is more efficient than the capitalist system in generating, mobilising and getting control of the economic surplus or for bringing about capital accumulation. To put it in a different way, the capitalist system will take a much longer time to reach a given level of capital accumulation than what would be taken by the communist system. To quote Joan Robinson:

> Compared to a purely feudal system, capitalism was a great invention for promotion of accumulation. It shifted the balance of power from property to enterprise and got going the process of accumulation. Compared to capitalism, socialism makes the transfer in a still more thorough-going way. Property ceases to exist, and the animal spirits of enterprise drive the whole economy to undertake unprecedented feats. Thus so far as underdeveloped economies are concerned, it seems that socialism is going to beat capitalism at its own game, and the reason that it will do so is a far more powerful instrument for extracting the investible surplus from an economy.

Thus, as far as extracting the investible surplus is concerned, the communist system is more efficient than the contemporary capitalist system. As the size of the investible surplus is an important determinant of the rate of economic growth, this gives the communist system an advantage over the capitalist system in bringing about economic growth. Additionally, the investment policy of the communist society is, as stated earlier, more geared to economic growth than that followed in a capitalist society.

However, it is not merely the size of the investible surplus or the manner in which the investible surplus is actually invested that determines economic growth. Economic growth also turns on the efficiency of the operation, and the productivity of labour in industry, agriculture, transport and in other sectors of the economy. Productivity of labour in general is higher in the capitalist societies than in the communist systems. This is because in the case of the capitalist system the individual is the basis and motivation is directed towards the individual; while in the case of the communist system, it is the community which is the basis, and motivation is directed towards the community functioning through its individuals in a mystic way under the leadership of the party. After all, productivity is not merely the result of having good technical skills; or of having modern machinery; or of having a favourable environment in terms of natural resources. Productivity is also the result of that little something which is the interest of the man concerned in bringing about the maximum production, his freedom to experiment, his freedom to make losses, his urge to express himself, his personality, his dynamism, his drive, his go-gettingness, his 'animal spirits', if one uses Joan Robinson's phrase in terms of economic activity. In the case of the capitalist system the producer does get motivated to a larger extent than is the case in the communist system. And that is one major reason why, though the rate of growth is higher in terms of investment goods in the communist system, productivity therein per unit of labour in agriculture and even in industry cannot compare with that in the advanced and developed capitalist societies.

Thus neither the capitalist nor the communist systems can claim to have all the advantages as instruments of economic development. Both have their good points; and both have their weaknesses. Neither of them is likely to replace the other and they have to reconcile themselves to each other's existence on a continuing basis. That is why the cold war has seemed so futile to a non-aligned observer who does not owe allegiance to either of these systems. Coexistence of the capitalist and communist systems thus gets its logical basis not only on the balance of military power and international alliances but also on the failure of either to hold the unique key to economic development. To quote Joan Robinson in regard to the rival claims of the capitalist and communist methods of economic development:[9]

> First I argued that the socialist system is well suited to the need of developing economies. Now I am maintaining that capitalism, if it is managed with intelligence and goodwill, may continue to flourish in economies that are already developed. If my argument is correct, we have to look forward to a long period of coexistence of different economic systems.

Some may go further than Ms. Robinson and question the very validity of maintaining and continuing a clear-cut distinction between the capitalist and communist systems of economic development. Capitalist economic development in its later stages, as during the last decade and even earlier, contains a number of features that have formed an essential part of the communist methods of economic development. And communist economic development in its later stages, as in the case of the Soviet Union in the post-Stalinist era, is increasingly incorporating features, that have formed as essential part of the capitalist methods of economic development. The capitalist system in the developed countries is going in for planning, diminished competition, concentration of decision making on vital economic issues in fewer and fewer hands, and increasingly diminishing play of volition and individual choice in determining the rate of saving and the pattern of investment. The communist system in the developed and even developing countries is, on the other hand, increasingly going in for decentralisation, motivation directed towards individuals, competition rephrased as emulsion, less un-free markets, and increasing use of incentives, inducements and stimulation rather than force, ideology, and administrative decrees. The capitalist and the communist systems are not showing any inhibition in taking from each other what they think will serve them better in the strategy of economic development and the promotion of economic growth; only they are not getting merged with each other. The lines are still separate but they are no longer at right angles to each other. It is true they are moving as parallel lines and hence the continuing co-existence of the two systems; but the two parallel lines are getting nearer each other and hence the coexistence will get easier as time passes. From narrow standpoint of mere economic growth, therefore, there is something more academic than practical in viewing them as two watertight alternative means to economic development.

There is another factor, which has not been mentioned so far, which is also tending to bring the two systems closer to each other in their operation; and that is the large and increasing place occupied by armaments and military preparedness, both defensive and offensive, in their economies. And in this respect, the two systems are not only moving on parallel lines but also getting closer to each other. Only this getting closer together is indicative not of a possible operation in the interests of a durable world peace even on a balance of power thesis. In fact, it is tending in the direction of a major confrontation, that will sooner or later, result in a global nuclear war that will destroy both as also the developing countries and their dreams of economic development. Recent international developments are strengthening this trend; and unless something drastic is done to strengthen the detentes, bring about a reduction in armaments, stop the extension of nuclear weapons either by placing or by domestic production, and eventually bring about a total disarmament in both conventional and nuclear armaments and military forces, all the talk about economic development or attempts at economic development by the less developed countries will only end in futility and become a part of the ashes of a third World War. The developing world cannot afford to see an armed clash between the Soviet Union and its allied powers and the United States and its allied powers, whether in the name of fighting capitalism or fighting communism or for narrow national interests or for prestige or power reasons. The developing countries have not only to choose between the capitalist or communist or other alternative methods of economic development but, more importantly, they have to go all out to prevent an outbreak of war between the super-powers either directly or by proxy that will put an end to their chance of having any economic development irrespective of the ideological form it may take. A basic pre-condition for the economic development of the less developed countries has thus become the prevention of a Third World War. And the only way the developing countries can do this is to avoid military alliances or entanglements with either of the super-powers or their proxies, not get drawn into the world of satellite or client states, and firmly proclaim and practise a policy of non-alignment and actively exert the moral influence thus acquired to get the super powers to sit together in dialogue and end their mutual confrontation by compromise and conciliation. To play the role of an honest broker between the super-powers has now become as much the task of the developing countries as their choice of a desired strategy for economic development and taking the necessary measures for their development. It is high time this is recognised and accepted by all persons interested in the economic development of the under-developed world, whether they belong to the western capitalist world or the communist eastern world or the ideologically miscellaneous mixture of the less developed Third World.

Mere economic growth, however, is no longer an exclusive economic objective. After all, economic growth is only means to an end, which is human welfare. And there can be no welfare without socíal justice. Removal of poverty and unemployment and minimisation (drastic or moderate, depending upon the economic system one is talking about) of inequalities in income and wealth and increasing equalisation of opportunities are now considered as imperative of economic development not only in socialist countries but also in Third World countries and by liberal opinion even in capitalist countries. This is particularly true of India, where the nationally accepted objective is economic growth with social jüstice. The comparative pull of communist and capitalist ideologies on the intellectuals of the Third World will therefore turn not only on their efficiency as instruments for economic growth but also on the extent to which they promote social justice as a part of the process of development.

The capitalist system has shed some of the unpleasant social features associated with its early history. Health, education, unemployment insurance, maternity benefits, leave with pay, restrictions on hours of work and ban on the employment of children, collective bargaining for wage determination and for wage increase in line with rise in the cost of living and in productivity, subsidisation of agricultural producers and some other benefits for members of the working classes are now to be found in many capitalist economies. The capitalist state is professedly turning into a welfare state and what is called people's capitalism is claimed to be replacing the old-fashioned exploitative capitalism of the nineteenth century. With all this, however, capitalist societies continue to be afflicted by unemployment, inflation and rising costs of living, and substantial differences in the real level of living between the many and the few. Capitalist enterprise still continues its international exploitative role, though the forms and techniques employed have changed. And giant multi-national corporations have become a new menacing feature whose unhealthy influence extends both within and across national frontiers. With the exception of a few small countries like Sweden, Denmark, Norway, Finland and New Zealand, the rest of the capitalist world still leaves a lot to be desired in terms of social justice, class barriers, and inequalities in income, wealth, and economic opportunities. Even such improvement as has taken place in the conditions of the working class and of the poor is due to the development based on the earlier exploitation within the continuing exploitation without. As such exploitation is neither desirable nor perhaps even possible for new entrants into the capitalist arena, it becomes a moot point whether capitalist enterprise and social justice can go together in newly developing capitalist economies and whether it is possible to change the face of capitalism in its early years of development. Capitalist development in the Third World has tended to lean on foreign capital and foreign know-how, and the dependence that follows is neither conducive to their needed economic growth nor to social justice for their working masses nor to eventual self-reliance. In fact it poses a threat even to national autonomy and freedom of choice for preferred forms of social development. Nor do the ills of affluence that pervade the contemporary capitalist world, the insecurity for further growth that is now leading to talk of the limits of growth, and the environmental damage they already suffer from, make for the acceptance of capitalism as a preferred social system to the idealist and the intellectual in the developing world.

The communist system, on the other hand does present an alternative picture from the point of view of social justice. It provides full employment, even if all employees do not get the employment of their individual choice. Prices of essential goods of mass consumption are held at stable levels and starvation is an unusual and unlikely phenomenon. Nor is there any distortion of demand and wasteful consumption stimulated by commercial advertisements. There is no fear of exploitation by private employers as there is no private employment. Though there is some inequality of income, its range is definitely less than in capitalist societies. In any case differences in levels of living of different sections are considerably less, and such luxury goods as are available are highly priced, while essential articles and cultural goods and services are subsidised and brought within the reach of the masses of the people. Communist systems are known for the priority they give to public transport over private transport, requirements of children over those of adults, and of mass consumption goods over less essential and luxury goods. There is hardly any conspicuous consumption by individuals, conspicuousness being confined to collective consumption which the masses can share. Recently the opening of the communist countries for tourist traffic, and the lifting of the iron curtain has brought about some change in the situation, but by and large, the communist countries still continue to have the better of the capitalist ones in terms of social justice and the material conditions of the masses in comparison to the better off sections of their population. It is this which constitutes its comparative advantage to many persons in the developing countries.

It is in respect of the political system and the individual freedoms it permits that the capitalist society exercises its greatest appeal to the intelligentsia in the developing countries. The capitalist system is distinguished from the communist system by its system of government responsibility to the legislature, secrecy of ballot, independent judiciary and multi-party system. Under the communist system, on the other hand, though there is adult franchise and periodic elections, there is only one political party and that is officially in charge of the state. Political power thus gets concentrated in the Communist party. Its leadership may change as a result of intra-party factions or policy differences, but the vast majority of the population who are not members of the party have no say in the choice of their rulers.

Then again, fundamental rights of the individual such as the freedom of speech, freedom of association, freedom of the press and freedom to strike found in capitalist democracies are not prevalent in the communist states. *Habeas corpus* and writ petitions and *suo motto* powers of the judiciary are conspicuous by their absence. The individual of course has the right to work and to a basic minimum livelihood, which do mean a great deal to the common man, and, according to some, are far more important than civil freedom.

Suppression of individual civil rights and freedom of expression do not constitute a part of communist ideology. The deviation in practice from the ideal is justified on the necessity of socialist countries having to fight for their very survival in a capitalist world which offers not only threats but also blandishments; and the prevailing constraints on individual freedom are explained away in terms of preventing domestic vested interests from following a line of action prejudicial to the survival of socialism. Attention is also drawn to the fact that civil freedoms which exist in capitalist countries, are, in general, enjoyed more by the classes rather than the masses, whose economic and educational inferiority prevents them from having effective recourse to their civil rights. With all this, however, no objective observer can fail to see the difference that exists in practice between communist and capitalist societies in regard to the civil liberties of the individual or the freedom given to the voice of dissent in a multi-party political system as compared to a single-party system. Nor can it be denied that civil freedoms and fundamental human rights not only form a part of the liberal heritage of western societies, but also of those developing countries of the Third World which have wrested their freedom from their western masters by making this heritage their own. This is certainly true of India which has shown by its post-independence political history its adherence to the liberal values of political democracy, individual freedom and independent judiciary.

The fundamental dilemma still remains however of how to reconcile economic growth with social justice, national self-reliance, and political democracy in a developing society. It is this dilemma which has to be faced and solved in any attempt to build a socialist society in India.

REEERENCES

1. For a more elaborate account of this process and its similarity under the capitalist and communist systems see, V.K R.V. Rao "Freedom and development : The challenge with special reference to India". *Journal of the Australian Institute of International Affairs*, August 1960.
2. See V.K.R.V. Rao, *op. cit*.
3. Japan is a notable exception to this thesis as far as its performance after World War II is concerned. Apart from its traditional habits

and national psychology, reaction to defeat in the second World War and increased industrial efficiency all contributed to this outcome.

4. I.A. Yevenko, Planning in the USSR, p. 126. Also compare the resolution on the subject passed at the 21st (Extraordinary) Congress of the Communist Party of the Soviet Union held in Moscow in 1969: "The Communist Party of the Soviet Union attaches paramount importance to the development of industry. particulaıly heavy industry, which is the foundation of foundations of Socialist economy and of the might of the country. Moreover, it is the decisive factor in the development of productive force and in the growth of labour productivity in all branches of the national economy".
5. I.A. Yevenka, Planning in the USSR, p. 108-9.
6. See Maurice Dobb, *Soviet Economic Development Since 1917*, Fourth Edition, p. 234.
7. W.G. Hoffman, *The Growth of Industrial Economies*, Bombay, Oxford University Press, 1958, p. 97.
8. Surendra J. Patel, "Rates of industrial growth" *Economic Development and Cultural Change*, Vol. 9, Pt. 2, April, 1961, pp. 316-330.
9. Joan Robinson, *Collected Economic Papers*, Vol. 2, Oxford, Basil Blackwell, 1964, p. 106.

The Democratic Socialist Alternative 3

DEMOCRATIC socialism is an alternative to communism or scientific socialism more in regard to the means adopted for the capture of political power and control over the state apparatus and the manner in which the state machinery is used for bringing socialism into existence rather than in regard to its economic programmes. But there is one significant difference on the economic side to which attention has to be drawn. Thus the socialist states based on Marxist-Leninist or Marxist-Leninist-Maoist ideology go in for public ownership of all means of production, distribution and exchange, while those based on the ideology of democratic socialism permit a limited measure of private ownership of means of production, distribution and exchange, while bringing under public ownership and operation or under public regulation the larger units of these fields. It is for this reason that states professing democratic socialism go in for what has come to be known as a mixed economy, while those adhering to a communist ideology go in for a fully socialised or cooperative economy. This difference, however, is not due so much to differences in economic reasoning as in political attitudes towards the nature of democracy, the role of the individual, the desirable balance of the power structure within the community, and the link assumed between economic activity and personal freedom.

Subject to these differences, there is a great deal in common between these two categories of socialist states in respect of their economic programmes that constitute their socialist operations. A socialist society has not only to bring about equitable distribution but also to maximise production. It has to solve the problems of unemployment, low income and mass poverty, and bring about a significant improvement in the national standards of living.

This is not possible without a substantial increase in the volume of investment. If the required increase in investment is to be brought about without stimulating inflation, there must be a corresponding significant rise in the rate of domestic saving. The needed increase in savings cannot be mobilised merely by tapping the surplus element in the larger incomes in a developing society. An appreciable contribution is also needed from the masses either by way of taxes or loans, even though, by absolute standards, they may have no surplus to contribute. This will not be easy in a poor country. It will be even more difficult if the country has a democratic set-up, where the poor who constitute the bulk of the electorate, do not have the normal minima for even basic necessities, and cannot expect any significant rise in their living standards in the immediate future in spite of the economic development they will be called upon to finance. What is needed, therefore, is some powerful motivation that will induce the masses to make the required contribution to the savings needed for economic development. The democratic socialist would be no better incentive for this purpose than the use of the savings contributed by the masses for building a socialist society. Secondly, any substantial measure of economic development requires not only an appreciable rise in the rate of savings and investment, but also a planned use of these savings in such a manner as to bring about an accelerated rate of economic growth. This requires an investment pattern that will be based not only on operational profits but also on social priorities in the pattern of output.

Socialism, therefore, requires deliberate and purposive action on the part of the state in regard to both production and distribution; and the fields covered are not only savings, investment, human skills and use of science and technology, but also changes in property relations, taxation, public expenditure, education and the social services. A socialist society is not just a give-away society nor is it only concerned with distribution of income. It must bring about full employment as also an increase in productivity. For doing this, it is necessary that the creative energies of the people are released, and talent everywhere gets the opportunity for development and social contribution. It is necessary that the community becomes scientific and technology-minded, and is willing to go in for the relevant changes in methods, practices, and organisation of production. It is also necessary that workers both in industry and agriculture, get the habit of workers in cooperation. The key-note of the socialist system is, from the economic point of view, a significant rise in productive efficiency on the part of the nation as a whole.

For securing this objective, a socialist society must necessarily transform the economic organisation of production, distribution, exchange and consumption in the community. As far as production is concerned, the primary motivation has to be a rise in living standards in the present, and a promise of a greater rise in the future. Production, therefore, has to be not for private profit but for public use, that is, emphasis will be on production of mass consumption or wage goods on the one hand, and capital goods on the other. This requires the planning of production by a central authority. Such centralised planning does not mean, however, centralised control of productive operations or centralised decision-making in regard to all types of economic activity. In fact, for countries of large size which have significant regional variations in resources, needs and skills, decentralisation of production is an essential condition for maximising the national output. At the same time, centralised action is required in regard to priorities in investment, mobilisation of resources, optimum utilisation of scarce supplies of both natural resources and special skills, and evaluation of performance. Thus, centralisation has to go hand in hand with decentralisation; and this has to take the form of co-ordination rather than control at the central level. It also follows that appropriate action has to be taken for securing the implementation of such a plan.

Such a transformation of production will not be possible in the absence of an appropriate change in the system of distribution of the economic product. These changes have to include the elimination of all types of unearned incomes, functionless receipts, monopoly profits, and the like. Functionless income will include not only rentier income, that is income which is not connected with work by the recipient, either in the present or in the past, but also income that is apparently functional but is really not so because of its exploitative character, such as monopoly profits. In a socialist society, work must always accompany income; and, at the same time, it will be part of the responsibility of the community to look after the needs of all those who cannot work.

This means that the organisation of trade will have to be different in a socialist community. There has always been a considerable measure of doubt about the social legitimacy of trading profits as compared with manufacturing profits; but one can see in a competitive and individualistic society some justification for remunerating the exercise of intelligence regarding the movement of goods over time or space. In a socialist society, however, conditions are entirely different. A socialistic society involves a planned economy which takes note of time and space considerations in the distribution and pricing of output. Private profits in wholesale trading would, therefore, be out of place in a socialist economy and wholesale trade will have to be reorganised on a cooperative or governmental basis.

Banking is another field which requires radical reorganisation in the context of a socialist society. In a socialist society, bank credit is required mainly for governmental or cooperative enterprise. If private enterprise continues to exist, the credit facilities extended to it will have to be regulated and rationed in the light of overall planning, nor can there be any privacy or bankers' secret about individual incomes or wealth. It would be necessary for both the efficient working of socialist enterprise and the preventing of unplanned and anarchical expansion of private enterprise that banking ceases to be under private ownership and/or management and is not only owned but also operated by the community.

The organisation of consumption will also be different in a socialist society. Consumer cooperatives will be preferable to private retail trading, but the choice between them will be voluntary and will rest on their comparative attractiveness to the consumer. There can be no doubt, however, that the price mechanism has to continue not only for the purpose of equating supplies and demands but also for giving freedom to the consumer in the utilisation of his disposable income and giving guidance to the planning organisation in the determination of the pattern of production. It is wrong to believe that the consumer will be a passive spectator in a planned economy. On the contrary, a truly socialist society will give freedom of choice to the consumer and, in fact to a much larger number of consumers than is the case in a capitalist society with its inequality of incomes, its manufacturing and trading monopolies or semi-monopolies, and its huge outlay on advertisement. Restrictions on consumer freedom will, however, be necessary in regard to expenditure of a wasteful or anti-social character, including luxury and display.

Then there is no question of the public versus the private sector. This is a crucial question in the interpretation of democratic socialism on which there is a great deal of misunderstanding among the general public. It is necessary to make it clear that a socialist society does not mean that every worker is an employee, nor does it mean that no economic activity can be organised on a private basis. What a socialist society requires is that no private individual or interest is able to influence either output or price in any given field and also that no private individual or interest has the power to exploit workers or acquire the surplus value generated by labour. In an ideal socialist society, people should either be self-employed, or if employed, be employed cooperatively or in socialist industry. It is therefore the scale and nature of economic activity that would determine the relative roles of the public and the private sector. This would mean that if the country has a vast number of small-sized production, trading, and service units, there would be a large scope for the private sector. And, even in the public sector, there should be ample scope for decentralised management and a certain measure of flexibility and dispersal of initiative in economic decision-making, depending upon the size of the country and its local and regional variations.

It is also wrong to think that normal economic incentives have no place in a socialist society. On the contrary, economic incentives need to be used, but their operation and incidence should be regulated in the light of the plan objectives, whereas they work in a haphazard and anti-social fashion in a capitalist society. No socialist society can merely rely on legislation or coercion for implementing its programme of production and capital formation. At best these can only have a negative effect. Speeches and exhortations can create a favourable atmosphere but cannot in themselves be a substitute for incentives. It is only incentives that can influence individual behaviour and it is individual behaviour and reaction to stimuli that determine to a large extent the efficiency of the national economic effort; hence the need for a close study of incentives in a socialist society. The only caution to be added is that incentvies need not only be monetary but can also be in terms of prestige, public appreciation, etc. Care should also be taken to see that, taking the totality of incentives, the overall balance is favourable, as a favourable incentive to one person or class may be accompanied by an opposite effect on another person or class.

A socialist order cannot be brought into existence without changing the institutional framework of the society in question, and these changes do not only relate to the organisation of economic activities like production, distribution, exchange and consumption. Changes have to be brought about in the basic institutions and values that govern economic and social growth. Thus, there has to be wholesale review of the rights of property and property relations. Property as an opportunity for the control of economic activity is basically inconsistent with a socialist system. Ideally property should be in private hands only for the purpose of consumption, means of production being socially owned if not actually socially operated in every case. Even if it is not possible to bring about such revolutionary change, it is essential that (a) property rights are severely limited and (b) ceilings are placed on individual property, and ownership of all property above those ceilings is transferred to the community at large. Ceilings on land in rural areas must have their counterpart in urban areas and this should take the form of the ceilings on property of all kinds in the country, whether landed or otherwise, whether owned by rural residents or by urban residents. Income may perhaps remain without a statutory ceiling; though obviously the tax burdens that income will bear will sharply increase with size and bring about a ceiling on personal incomes in practice.

A second set of institutional changes relates to the operation of the public sector. With all the socialist sentiment that we can stimulate, the fact remains that human nature by and large tends to give a higher place to personal over public interest. When a large share of the means of production, distribution and exchange are publicly-owned and operated by persons who are only employees, two sets of difficulties arise in regard to their efficient operation. One is the freezing role of bureaucratisation and the other a dimunition of hard work, discipline, and responsibility on the part of individual employees. The problem of combining centralisation with flexibility and control with initiative arise in the case of large undertakings even in a capitalist society based on private property and operated on the profit motive. It arises even more in a socialised economy wtth a centralised planning machinery and its attendant bureaucracy, as the Soviets have found in spite of their one-party system and the extensive control and influence exercised by the party over all aspects of national life. The problem is even more serious when the large public sector has to operate under a system of parliamentary democracy, where ministerial accountability and bureaucratic power both combine to sap initiative and flexibility on the part of individual undertakings. This is the field where a new managerial revolution is required. Institutional changes need to be brought about in the control and operation of the public sector that will combine maximum efficiency on the part of individual units with maximum translation of the social purpose in their operations. In spite of all the work that the Soviet Union has put in this field, a satisfactory solution is not yet in sight; and it is bound to be more difficult for developing countries which choose to follow the path of democratic socialism. The other problem confronting the public sector is in respect of its non-managerial personnel who are still to find a sense of identification with the units in which they work, though theoretically they run it collectively as citizens of a socialist state. There has been a great deal of talk and some experimentation with devices like worker participation, profit-sharing, production-bonus, socialist emulation, etc., but so far no satisfactory way has been found to make the worker in a public enterprise function as he would in a production unit of which he was a personal owner. All that can be said in this context is that here is a field of socialist technology of management and worker motivation that is badly in need of institutional change. Obviously, both the carrot and the stick have a role to play in this matter; and so also adaptation to socialist requirements of techniques operated with success in capitalist enterprises and economies. Only the thinking on the subject and experience gained so far do not appear sufficient to outline in concrete terms what should be the nature of the institutional change that production units need in the context of their having to operate in the public sector.

A third set of institutional changes that a socialist economy requires in respect of public finance, resources mobilisation and public expenditure. The problem is not identical for a developed economy that has taken to the socialist path and a developing economy that is seeking to build a socialist society. For the latter—and this would apply to a country like India—backwardness has to be conquered and simultaneously equity has to permeate the entire economy. The phrase used by Indian leadership to describe the objective is "economic growth with social justice". What it means in practice is maximum resource mobilisation for utilisation under public ownership, control or guidance for the twin purpose of promoting economic growth and meeting the imperative needs of the poor and the disadvantaged in the community in terms of their levels of living, opportunities for advancement, and reduction in the disparities in income, wealth and economic power. Taxation, savings, prices, deficit financing and profits of public enterprises, all these constitute a part of the technology of resource mobilisation, while maximisation of employment, special treatment of the disadvantaged, regulation of wages, equalisation of educational and income earning opportunities. and public provision or subsidisation of social services constitute a part of the technology of imparting social justice to the economy. To what extent these two technologies of socialist transformation are competitive or complementary, what their relations are in the short period and the long period, and the extent and the manner in which they need to be phased out over time are all questions on which thinking is insufficiently developed so far, and particularly so in the case of parliamentary democracies seeking economic development through a socialist path or backward economies which want to become practitioners of democratic socialism. What is clear in this context is the imperative need for active mass participation in a deliberate and purposive manner in the process of socialist transformation with all that it implies in terms of hard work, discipline, savings, identification of the appropriate priorities between the present and the future, and ability to understand and accept the practical reality of the difference between tactics and strategy for socialist transformation. What we now need is not so much a theory of socialist capture of power as a theory of socialist use of power or of socialist transformation under a parliamentary democracy. Such a theory has not been evolved in the west and it is still to be evolved elsewhere.

A fourth set of institutional changes that socialism and particularly democratic socialism requires is the socialising of the economic activity that is still permitted to operate under private property and individual enterprise in a mixed economy. Soviet leadership tried to solve this problem by abolishing all elements of mixed economy in production and by trying to industrialise agricultural production on the factory pattern. Their grand attempt at collective farming has still to yield worthwhile results in terms of maximisation of production, while the extent to which it has been able to eliminate what it calls the bourgeois psychology from agriculture is still a matter of grave doubt for objective observers. In fact abandonment of collective farming in some of the East European communist countries and tolerance of the elements of personal holdings among members of collective farms even in the Soviet Union are all pointers to the difficulty of reconciling the ideological objectives behind socialising agriculture with the economic objective of maximising production. In parliamentary democracies with free and periodic elections, where there are literally millions of production units not only in agriculture but also in industries, trade and the services, it is almost impossible to socialise such economic activity. That is why mixed economy has been accepted as a part of democratic socialism. At the same time we cannot ignore the bourgeois roots that a mixed economy generates and the very real possibility of their overpowering the socialist nature of the society we are seeking to build. From the point of view of pure socialist theory, a mixed economy is not only an anachronism but also a danger to socialist survival; and yet from the practical point of view we cannot escape a mixed economy for parliamentary democracies, however strong may be the socialist commitment for their leadership, when this leadership rests on electoral support and has to face the daily press and periodic elections. What we need, therefore, is a set of institutional devices that will dilute the bourgeois character of privately owned and operated units in a mixed economy; and simultaneously, eternal vigilance is needed in guarding against extension to the public sector of the individualistic psychological influences emerging from the private sector.

A fifth set of institutional changes relates to the whole field of education from the primary to the university level. The entire system of education in the country will have to be reviewed from a socialist angle, with one of its basic objectives being the creation of understanding, acceptance and preparedness to work for a socialist society among the pupils. This is not easy to achieve, nor can it be done within a short period. This has to be done with great skill, for what is wanted is not just propaganda but education. Propaganda is like hypnotism; its effect is purely temporary and its aftermath usually ends in a reaction against the initial effects. What is needed is education that exposes the teaching to discussion and debate and, if correct, ends in a conviction that acquires an enduring base in both individuals and society. Such education for socialism has to be given on both the intellectual and the emotional planes for winning acceptance by the community at large of the new social order. And that means a near-revolutionary change in the educational system.

The changes we need in the educational system should include three essential elements if they are to sustain both the production and the distribution aspects of a socialist society. These are: (i) equalisation of opportunities and special measures for dealing with the handicap of backwardness; (ii) understanding of science and technology not merely as subjects for academic study but as a way of life; and (iii) inculcation of a feeling of social responsibility and identification with mass welfare that will produce the psychological foundation needed for socialist behaviour. Maximum attention should be paid to children, not only in respect of education but also of nutrition and medical care. It is the disparities in education, nutrition and medical care that are largely responsible for the inequalities that emerge when the child grows to adulthood. Hence a children's charter is a *sine qua non* of the foundations of a socialist society. This fact has won recognition in the Soviet Union and, whatever other criticisms one may offer on life in the Soviet Union none can deny the primacy of attention that children get in that country. Pre-school and primary education should, therefore be completely reoriented under democratic socialism to offer all children equal opportunity in terms of education, food and good health. Simultaneously, the system should provide for special training programmes for children who are handicapped by their economic or social or other cirumstances from taking full advantage of the facilities offered by the educational system. It is also important that not merely the content but the method of instruction followed is such that a scientific outlook and ability to use tools becomes an integral part of the educational system and a way of life for those who pass through its portals. And finally, education should become synonymous with a humane outlook, a sense of social identification, and a desire to make the best of oneself and share it with the rest of society. All these desiderata of socialist education cannot come without a fundamental restructuring of the educational system in terms of numbers, vocation, access, staffing, equipment, methodology, of instruction, integration with the community and social purpose. Education of the type mentioned will of course be expensive, but cheap education cannot produce socialist ethos either in terms of equality or of productivity. In fact, it is the educational system that a socialist country provides for its children and youth that would determine its survival in trems of emotional acceptance and operational efficiency.

Democratic socialism, with its emphasis not only on equality but also on productivity and economic growth requires an appropriate use of science and technology by the socialist society. This requires not only the creation of science laboratories and technological institutions, but also a place for science in non-science courses in schools and colleges and the strengthening of university departments of science for the promotion of fundamental research. It also requires work experience on the part of both teachers and students in technological institutions, as also continuing education in both science and technology to keep the community up-to-date in its knowledge. Above all, a modern society is not only an industrial society that makes use of science and technology in its manufacture, transport, and other infrastructural activities, but also makes use of science and technology in all aspects of its life. This needs therefore the creation of a scientific climate in this country and a scientific temper among its people and not just the setting up of institutions of science and technology and facilities for instruction in those subjects. Research and Development or R & D as it is called, is also a fundamental aspect of the use of science and technology in a modern industrial society, the responsibility for which rests on all those engaged in productive activity on a scale sufficient to warrant it, whether in the public or the private sector.

The important point to note in connection with these institutional changes is that they cannot be brought into effect merely by legislation or governmental pressures. What is needed is intensive education both on a national scale and on an individual basis combined with a trained body of cadres who would both educate the people and operate the changed institutions. Cadre building is much easier in a communist state with a one party system and an almost complete lack of distinction between the official and the party workers in terms of power, prestige and levels of living and admitting of a continuous inflow and outflow of personnel between them. Similarly, education as a defined ideology becomes easier in a totalitarian state with monopolistic control over all media of communication. For a socialist leadership functioning under parliamentary democracy, the problem of providing the ballast and the dynamics for institutional change is much more difficult. There is a sharp and conspicuous distinction between party workers in the organisation and party workers in the ministry nor is there anything like free or continuous inflow and outflow among them. Unless this is remedied by conventions making for inter-change between the organisational and ministerial wings of political parties, it would be difficult to build the cadres needed for maintaining continuous contact between people and government. Nor can socialist education be brought about by control of the press and other media of communication. In any case, freedom of speech and press is a part of the democratic way of life and an essential ingredient of socialism. What really stands in the way of socialist education for producing a socialist is not the want of precept and profession, but that of example; and for that it is the leadership that is to blame and not the working of democracy. What we fail to realise is that democratic socialism requires in its leaders a larger degree of dedication to socialist ideology, evidenced by their life and conduct, a closer nearness to the common people by actual personal contact, a greater willingness on their part to exchange office for party work, and an intellectual concern with the concrete problems of socialist transformation. With this would be combined willingness to share unpleasant facts with the people and courage to court unpopularity in the larger interests of the socialist purpose of maximising production and equalising distribution.

In truth, while democratic socialism is superior to the so-called scientific socialism or currently practised communism in term of both of its human content and the chances of long-term survival, its path to success is strewn with far more difficulties and calls for a much greater degree of skill, dedication, persuasiveness and personal example in its leadership than is the case with communism. Democratic socialism does not envisage abolition of private property in all means of production or distribution or exchange but allows for the simultaneous existence of an extensive private sector along with a growing public sector, the private sector being regulated in the social interest, while the public is expected to play a socialist role both by its direct participation in economic activity and the use it makes of the commanding heights it occupies in the economy.

Democratic socialism, therefore, operates through a mixed economy unlike the Russian, Chinese and East European economies where there is no more than a marginal place, if any, for the private sector. Politically, democratic socialism works within a parliamentary democracy and a multi-party system without any monopolistic advantage for the ruling party and with the inevitable constraints springing from freedom of speech, association and press. Inevitably, therefore, this throws much greater responsibility for persuasive and effective leadership on the party or parties working for a democratic socialist society than is the case in socialist countries with a totalitarian political system, where the leadership faces no opposition from without and has only to deal with intrigues from within. Then again, the very constraints that democracy imposes on socialist transformation calls for more courage, more compromise, more sacrifice, and more effective and understanding leadership than is the case with communist parties that follow the path of class war, hatred, violence and proletarian dictatorship to establish the socialist society of their conception.

The most important implication of democratic socialism is the enormous responsibility it places for its implementation on the elite in its society. Having ruled out violence for the establishment of a socialist society and dictatorship for its maintenance, the democratic socialist has to fall back upon education, persuasion and self-sacrifice, besides of course, control over the governmental machinery obtained through democratic consent.

While a socialist society is attuned to mass welfare and egalitarian ideals, it cannot wipe out natural differences in ability, drive and qualities of leadership. Equalisation of opportunities cannot bring about arithmetical uniformity of equality; it can only give opportunities to enable ability and talent to grow and develop in spite of possible initial handicaps of caste, creed, poverty and social backwardness. While the poor may not always be with us, the elite will be, though their class composition would be different in a socialist society. And as, by definition, the elite will be in a position of power, influence and responsibility, it is essential that they be truly imbued with socialist faith, be motivated by socialist psychology, and function in both their official and personal lives as social trustees of the power or influence that their superior talents and training give them. This is particularly necessary in India, where the backlog of illiteracy and poverty is immense and the elite are small in number, and where therefore a very heavy burden will rest on this limited elite for bringing about socialist transformation. While educational reform will help in this process, other ways and means will have to be found to carry forward through the post-education and working period of their lives this special sense of mission and responsibility that democratic socialism requires from the elite.

This means that those who have money, brain or power—what may broadly be termed the privileged strata in society—have to adopt the gandhian way for leading and operating the socialist movement. The gandhian spirit has to permeate their being. The masses are the beneficiaries. It is the privileged classes who ought to feel a sense of dedication. This is the fundamental requirement for the establishment of a socialist society through democratic means. In other words, quite apart from what is done by way of legislation or administrative action, we need voluntary ceilings on income, voluntary restraints on money incentives, and greater importance for non-monetary incentives. What democratic socialism needs is something of the spirit of a religious mission, where leaders function as missionaries and treat their work as dedication, the rewards for which are not counted in terms of either money or power. If those who constitute its leadership, will only acquire this spirit and function not only through speeches, legislation and use of the state apparatus, but also through their personal life, sacrifices and example, the future is bright indeed for democratic socialism all over the world. The socialist state personnel, both political and bureaucratic, have a special obligation in this respect, as by the very nature of the case, large scale private enterprise will be playing a minor, if not negligible role, in a socialist society.

Democratic socialism also requires the development of participant democracy at all levels of collective functioning, whether at the political or economic or social levels. Local self-government, Panchayat Raj, co-operative societies, worker participation and voluntary agencies in fields of social or cultural interest are all necessary institutions for stimulating individual interest and collective action and constitute the framework of a truly socialist society. The great danger that confronts a socialist society is centralisation of power in government, the ruling party, and the bureaucracy; and the only way in which it can be countered is by strengthening democracy at the grass-roots, and giving opportunities to people at local levels to participate in decision-making and implementation in the economic and social fields. This in turn requires that illiteracy is abolished, education in civic rights and duties and understanding of the implications of local development universalised, and encouragement given to the right kind of leadership to emerge and function at local levels.

To sum up, a society can claim to be a democratic socialist society only if the economic system is based not on private ownership in basic means of large-scale production but on social ownership of such basic means of production and social appropriation of the surpluses. By ruling out the principle of private property in large scale means of production and therefore of large private profits, the socialist system eliminates the economic basis for the existence of class exploitation. By affirming the social character of appropriation and not merely social ownership of means of production, it also guards against the emergence of new forms of economic exploitation whereby the ruling party or the bureaucracy covertly or overtly appropriates the fruits of labour of the working classes. The implications of the democratic approach to socialism are to be found largely in the significant and far-reaching changes they call for in the social and institutional framework of the country on the one hand and in the radical transformation they require in the behaviouristic pattern and way of life of all sections of people from the political, economic and professional elite to the workers and peasants that constitute the masses. This is because of the greater possibilities of internal discord and even conflict under democratic socialism where the compulsions of economic development have to operate under conditions of civil freedom and regard for the individual. This is so especially for developing countries with their problems of poverty, unemployment and backwardness of large sections of their population. In fact economic development under democratic socialism is a part of total development. Total development is always more demanding in its calls, both positive and negative, on the leadership entrusted with this task. It also requires more positive action on the part of the individual in such a society. Hence the need for socialist education not only for the leadership but also for the people whom they lead on the path of social and economic change. It is in this call for greater and more positive individual response on the part of both leaders and followers that the challenge of the democratic approach to socialism lies.

Socialism through Trusteeship 4
The Gandhian Alternative

IF GANDHI can be called a socialist, it must be added that he was a most unorthodox one, for his economic norms cannot be found in any economic textbook, whether capitalist or communist. Addressing a college Economic Society as far back as 1916, Gandhi asserted: "I venture to think that the scriptures of the world are safer and sounder treatises of laws of economics than many of the modern books".[1] He drew no distinction between economics and ethics. Thus, in 1921, he wrote: "Economics that hurts the moral well-being of an individual or a nation is immoral, and, therefore, sinful".[2] He repeated his belief in 1924: "That economics is untrue which ignores or disregards moral values".[3] Writing thirteen years later, in 1937, he put in more content in his concept of economics:

> True economics never militates against the highest ethical standard, just as all true ethics to be worth its name must at the same time be also good economics. An economics that inculcates Mammon worship, and enables the strong to amass wealth at the expense of the weak, is a false and dismal science. It spells death. True economics, on the other hand, stands for social justice, it promotes the good of all equally, including the weakest, and is indispensable for decent life.[4]

This profound concern for the ethical ordering of economic life led him to pronounce a number of norms in the economic field. Thus, contrary to all accepted economic thinking, Gandhi denounced the principle of the unlimited character of human wants as the determinant of economic activity and its satisfaction as the index of economic progress:

> I do not believe that multiplication of wants and the machinery contrived to supply them is taking the world a single step nearer its goal. . . . I wholeheartedly detest this desire to destroy distance and time, to increase animal appetites and go to the ends of the earth in search of their satisfaction. If modern civilization stands for all this, and I have understood it to do so, I call it satanic.[5]

He was, of course, all in favour of an economic system that gave all human beings the means to satisfy their minimum material requirements. But he was not prepared to accept the thesis of the need for satisfying increasing human wants with its concomitant corollaries of more of machinery, industrialism and urbanism. "The mind is a restless bird", he observed, "the more it gets the more it wants and still remains unsatisfied". "Therefore", he went on, "the ideal of creating an unlimited number of wants and satisfying them seems to be a delusion and a snare".[6] And he concluded, "Civilisation in the real sense of the term, consists not in the multiplication but in the deliberate and voluntary reduction of wants".

Gandhi's opposition to the multiplication of wants was also linked to his love of the Indian village and its traditional way of life and his feeling that industrialisation on a mass scale would "necessarily lead to passive or active exploitation of the villagers as the problems of competition and marketing come in".[7] Throughout his life, Gandhi was drawn by his vision of a rural civilisation, where men and women in small groups would, by their activity, be self sufficient in meeting their elemental needs and yet inter-dependent for many others in which dependence is a necessity. "Under my scheme", he asserted, "nothing will be allowed to be produced by the cities which can equally well be produced by villages. The proper function of cities is to serve as clearing houses for village products".[8] In fact, the passion that lay behind his opposition to what he called "industrialism" was mainly the result of his desire to protect and sustain the village republics of his thinking. Decentralisation, both political and economic, was the core of his long and sustained thinking on the desired economic set-up, and behind it lay his conviction that only thus would the individual get free play for the expression and fulfilment of his personality.

There is no doubt that in this strong reaction against modern industrial civilisation and his idealisation of the village as the basis of a good society, Gandhi was largely influenced by the distress and pauperisation he had seen in Indian villages and the desperate exodus to urban areas that this had brought about, all largely as a result of the impact of modern industry brought into India under British rule in the form of imports and capitalist ideas of law, property, and competition. This was the reason why he responded so sympathetically to the tirade against an industrial civilisation that he read in the works of Thoreau, Ruskin, and Tolstoy. It all seemed to fit in so well with what he had seen happening to his own people; and more important still it also appeared to confirm the wisdom of the traditional preference of Hindu religion for austerity, renunciation, and involvement with matters of the spirit rather than with insatiable material craving. The fact that normal men and women were not inclined to reduce their wants except under compulsion made no difference to his conviction. The ethical imperative held sway over the economic reality and, as always, he was prepared to walk alone, provided he felt he was walking in the right direction. It must also be conceded that his theory of limitation of wants provided a logical basis for his economic thinking that frowned on industrialisation and urbanism and sought to make man rather than the machine the prime instrument of production.

Gandhi's attitude to the machine was perhaps the most controversial aspect of his economic thinking. Initially, Gandhi based his opposition to the machine on his reading of what was needed to constitute individual human happiness. "God created man to eat his bread by the sweat of his brow", he declared, "and I dread the prospect of our being able to produce all that we want, including our foodstuffs, out of a conjurer's hat".[9] He asserted: "It is only when a man or woman has done bodily labour for the sake of service that he or she gets any right to live".[10] He scoffed at the idea that the world could be divided into two categories of workers, intellectual and manual, and laughed at the artificial means of physical exercise that non-manual workers had to resort to for the sake of their health and digestion. No better apostle could be found for the gospel of manual work than Gandhi, who both preached and practised what he preached.[11]

Soon, however, Gandhi realised that his antipathy to the machine was being misunderstood, and more was being read into what he had said than was really meant. He asserted his readiness to make intelligent exceptions for permitting the use of machinery, his criteria for making the exceptions being where the machine helped the individual and did not encroach upon his individuality. "But simple tools and instruments, and such instruments and machinery as save individual labour and lighten the burden of the millions of cottagers, I should welcome".[12] Developing his thesis further, he argued that machinery had no place as long as there were unemployed persons who could not get work even with their hands, and asserted that he was against large-scale production only of those things that villagers can produce without diffiiculty. He gave balance to his views on machinery when he wrote in 1934: "Mechanisation is good when the hands are too few for the work intended to be accomplished. It is an evil when there are more hands than required for the work, as is the case in India. The problem with us is not how to find leisure for the teeming million inhabitants of our villages. The problem is how to utilise their idle hours, which are equal to the working days of six months in the year".[13] He was even more explicit four years later:

> If I could produce all my country's wants by means of 30,000 people instead of 30 million, I should not mind it, provided that the thirty million are not rendered idle and unemployed.[14]

If Gandhi had used economic jargon, he would have talked of the menace of technological unemployment or the need for labour-intensive methods of production in a country with abundant labour. He was only drawing attention to a problem which still remains to be solved in India, namely its massive unemployment which in fact has continued to grow after his death, in spite of nearly twenty-seven years of planned economic development.

Gandhi's objection to the extension of machinery was not based only on its relevance to unemployment in countries with surplus labour or its cramping effects on human personality even in the countries which had shortage of labour. He was also influenced by the implication of machinery and large-scale production on social justice. He was convinced that, under mechanised industry, the many will be exploited for the benefit of the few. "I can have no consideration for machinery which is meant to enrich the few at the expense of the many", he declared.[15] "Nor would there be any room in his picture of Indian independence for machines that would concentrate power in a few hands".[16] Answering in the affirmative a question whether he was opposed to machinery only because and when it concentrates production and distribution in the hands of the few, Gandhi replied: "I hate privilege and monopoly. Whatever cannot be shared with the masses is taboo to me".[17]

While Gandhi was thus trying to give economic and political reasoning support of his thesis against machinery, he was also undergoing a progressive change in his own attitude to a more extensive use of machinery in economic activity, even in his own beloved country. "I do visualise", he declared in 1940, "electricity, shipbuilding, iron works, machinemaking and the like existing side by side with village handicrafts. Hitherto industrialisation has been so planned as to destroy the village and the village crafts. In the state of the future, it will subserve the villages and their crafts".[18] He believed that it was possible to harmonise cottage industries and big industries if the latter are so planned as to help the villagers.[19] He was also not against centralisation of key industries provided this did not come in the way of the villager going in for it when he could do so with a little organising. Taking paper making in villages as an example, he declared that "supposing the State controlled paper making and centralised it, I would expect it to protect all the paper that villages can make".[20] He was also willing to accept the use of heavy machinery in the economy. "The heavy machinery for work of public utility, which cannot be undertaken by human labour, has its inevitable place", he conceded, but added, "but all that would be owned by the State and used entirely for the benefit of the people".[21] Thus step by step, Gandhi moved away from the initial position that he had taken that could not record a single good point in connection with machinery to a position where he conceded the place of machine, electric power, large industries, and key industries in the economy. Only he subjected this acceptance to several conditions. They must not deprive people of their employment, they must not exploit the villages or compete with village crafts, they must help the village artisan to reduce his drudgery and improve his efficiency. They should not tend to make atrophied the limbs of man. They must not lead to monopoly or concentration of wealth power in the few hands and they must not lead to exploitation, either national or international. And, when involving large capital or larger number of employees, they must be owned by the state and administered wholly for the public good. Truly a formidable list of qualifications, but no longer clouded either by references to 'sin' or the mysticism that put off so many intellectuals from his attitude to machinery and industrialisation. Gandhi's final theoretical position in regard to the machine and modern industry may best be summed up by quoting his own words:

> As a moderately intelligent man, I know that man cannot live without industry. Therefore I cannot be opposed to industrialisation. But I have a great concern about introducing machine industry. The machine produces much too fast, and brings with it a sort of economic system that I cannot grasp, I do not want to accept something when I see its evil effects which outweigh whatever good it brings with it. I want the dumb millions of our land to be healthy and happy, and I want them to grow spiritually. As yet for this purpose we do not need the machine. There are too many idle hands. But as we grow in understanding if we feel the need for machines, we certainly will have them. Once we have shaped our life on *Ahimsa*, we shall know how to control the machine.[22]

The development of Gandhian socialism can be seen in the central place he gave to full employment and the strong opposition he voiced to the use of machinery for exploiting human labour producing concentration of economic power. The basic convictions he held on the illegitimacy of private property and on the need for economic equality also constituted a major part of Gandhian socialism.

Speaking at the Guildhall in London on 22 September 1931, Gandhi said, "possession seems to me to be a crime. I can only possess certain things when I know that others who also want to possess similar things, are able to do so. But we know that such a thing, that can be possessed by all, is non-possession, not to have anything whatosoever".[23] Even Proudhon's famous statement "Property is theft", is not more drastic than this categorical pronouncement of Gandhi on the complete immorality of possessing any kind of property. This denial of the very concept of private property stemmed from his belief that all riches not only material but also physical and intellectual, belonged to God, and could be held by the individual only as a trust. Gandhi, of course, conceded the right of the individual to possession that would secure him the elemental necessities of life, but added "that even for this the condition of enjoyment or use of the necessities of life is their dedication. And that dedication or renunciation has got to be done from day to day, lest we may in this busy world forget the central fact of life".[24]

He was also fond of repeating a Hindu verse of sacred origin which has become current among the common people and could be translated as under: "All land belongs to Gopal where then is the boundary line: Man is the maker of that line and he can therefore unmake it." Gopal is one of the many names that the Hindus use when meditating on God. There could have been no better formulation of the thesis that property is a social concept and was therefore subject to change at the instance of society. Only Gandhi derived the concept from his religious reasoning and not from the facts of socio-economic history favoured by mundane economic historians and sociologists. Gandhi drew support for his thesis not only from the Hindu scripture, but also from all the known scriptures of the world. The categorical position taken up in his own as well as other scriptures about the limitations, if not the very denial, of the right of private property made him feel that this ought to satisfy all the cravings of the socialists and the communists who were so much against the principal of private property.[25] Gandhi equated private property in excess of the basic needs of human existence with exploitation; and it was this distrust of private property that made him proclaim several times that he was a socialist and a communist, though he was also quick to repudiate the other aspects of these creeds.

Side by side with this repudiation of private property, Gandhi also proclaimed his profound belief in the rightness of economic equality. He applied the principle not only to material property but also to the intelligence, skills, and other productive attributes of human beings that constituted their inseparable private property. He gave explicit formulation to these ideas when he said: "My ideal of socialism is that everyone should get the same wages. A lawyer, a physician, a teacher, a labourer or a sweeper—all should get equal wages".[26] He conceded that "Indian society may never reach that goal, but it is the duty of every Indian to set his soul towards that goal and no other, if India is to be a happy land".[27] Thus, Gandhi's ideas on economic equality were more extreme than those of the socialists who concentrated their attention on the economic inequalities resulting from private property and ignored those resulting from differences in human skills or responsibilities. In fact, he made a sharp distinction between contribution and retention, and said that "economic equality of my conception does not mean that everyone would literally have the same amount. It simply means that everybody should have enough for his or her needs. The real meaning of economic equality is: 'To each according to his needs.' That is the definition of Marx".[28]

Gandhi was fully aware of the vast gulf that lay between the contemporary economic, social, and political reality, and what he called the socialism of his conception. He knew how the latter needed for its implementation changes of a tremendous dimension to be brought about in the social order. He was, however, completely opposed to the use of either hatred or violence for bringing about social change. In fact, apart from their being wrong in themselves, he did not believe, that they would ever succeed in establishing an enduring socialist society. This did not mean, however that he accepted the existing social order.

On the contrary, he was certain that "a violent and bloody revolution is a certainty one day unless there is a voluntary abdication of riches and the power that riches give and sharing them for the common good".[29] When the second World War was at a critical stage, he wrote in his weekly:

> I have visions that the end of this war will mean also the end of the rule of the capital. I see coming the day of the rule of the poor, whether that rule be through force of arms or of non-violence. Let it be remembered that physical force is transitory, even as the body is transitory. But the power of the spirit is permanent, even as the spirit is everlasting.[30]

Thus, he shared with the Marxists their belief in the inevitability of the end of capitalism and agreed that socialism was the coming social order; but he did not accept their thesis that class war and violence were the only possible midwives of fundamental social change. Nor did he believe that such a change could be permanent if brought about by violence. For bringing about an enduring change, Gandhi believed that use had to be made of education, persuasion, love and non-violence. Declaring that "socialism is as pure as crystal",[31] and therefore needed crystal-like means to achieve it, he asserted that truth and *Ahimsa* must incarnate in socialism, and proclaimed his faith thus: "This I do say fearlessly and firmly, that every worthy object can be achieved by the use of *Satyagraha*. It is the highest and infallible means, the greatest force. Socialism will not be reached by any other means".[32]

With *Satyagraha* as the means and socialism as the objective to be achieved, Gandhi offered an alternative to the class war and proletarian dictatorship that communists and scientific socialists had espoused as the only means for the achievement of what they called socialism. The difference lay not only in the means to the followed. Inevitably, it also extended to the content of the objective itself. For Gandhi's socialism was not limited by class constraints. He believed in a classless society but did not think that this involved the destruction of the individuals who constituted the propertied classes. He was not prepared to identify capitalism with capitalists nor agrarian exploitation with landlords, even as he was not prepared to identify Englishmen as individuals with British rule. He was a believer in the essential unity of man. He fought the British on the political plane but was not prepared to see a single Britisher hurt or destroyed. Even so with capitalism; what he wanted to destroy was the system, and not the individuals who constituted its unjust beneficiaries. His goal was *Sarvodaya*, the welfare of all; and this included not only the humble and the lowly, and the lost, but also the capitalist and the landlord. The capitalist had to foreswear the use of capital for his personal ends, the landlord must give up the land in excess of his basic needs, and the exploited must be taught the strength that comes from non-cooperation with the exploiter, but all men had an equal right to life and the necessities of life. It was therefore that he declared : "And if I would recognise the fundamental equality, as I must, of the capitalist and the labourer, I must not aim at his destruction. I must strive for his conversion".[33] The language was the same that he had used with the foreign rulers of his country. In fact, it was the same language that he used with all those whom he regarded as either holding an unjust position or acting unjustly. The target of attack was always the system and never the man behind the system. The objective was conversion, and not physical destruction; the means was *Satyagraha* and not violence. Gandhi believed that it was possible through non-violence to transform the existing relationship between the classes and the masses into something healthier and purer and he could not subscribe to any social order, however good it was in other respects, that did not conform to his fundamental conviction in truth and non-violence. In the gandhian dictionary it is impossible to distinguish between means and ends; and therefore Gandhi's conception of socialism was basically different from that associated with communism or scientific socialism or the Russian experiment or now the Chinese experiment. Gandhi's socialism therefore cannot be treated as a first or even a second cousin of Marxian socialism. It is, in spite of similarities in some of the end-products envisaged in both, quite clearly and categorically an alternative to Marx and Lenin, Stalin and Mao.

The gandhian alternative is *Sarvodaya*, a classless society based on destruction of the class but not on the destruction of individuals who constitute the classes, a system of production that makes use of science and technology for creating an economy of abundance but does not in the process either kill individual initiative or freedom for development nor create a psychology of ceaseless striving for more and more of material goods, a system of distribution that will ensure a reasonable minimum income for all and, while not aiming at a universal equality of an arithmetical kind, will nevertheless ensure that all private property or talent beyond the minimum will be used as a trust for the public good and not for individual aggrandisement, a social order where all will work but there is no inequality either in status or in opportunity for any individual, and a political system where change is the result of persuasion, differences are resolved by discussion, and conflicts by love and recognition of mutuality of interest.

He did not, however, visualise a world where there will be no private property.[34] Only he would restrict it to what was necessary to yield an honourable livelihood, while for the excess he prescribed the principle of trusteeship. He invited the capitalist to regard himself as a trustee for those on whom he depends for the making, retention, and increase of his capital. He asked those who own property or skills to behave like trustees holding their riches on behalf of the poor. As trustees, they will be allowed to retain the stewardship of their possessions and to use their talent, to increase the wealth, not for their own sakes, but for the sake of the nation, and, therefore, without exploitation. The state will regulate the rate of commission which they will get commensurate with the service rendered and its value to society. As regards succession, while the first trustee could name his successor, it would be the state that would have the right of finalisation.

Gandhi evolved this theory of trusteeship not only on his deep religious conviction that everything belongs to God and therefore a human being can hold either his property or talent only as a trustee, but also on a number of practical considerations. He knew that to dispossess the man of property or of talent by force was bound to involve class war, hatred, proletarian dictatorship, an all-powerful and coercive state, and the consequent elimination of all hope of creating a non-violent society. He also felt that many men who had acquired property had some special abilities for increasing production and many men of talent had exceptional contributions to make, and, therefore, to destroy them by force, may lead to much less of production and would be like killing the goose that lays the golden eggs. Hence his emphasis on persuading them to function as trustees rather than dispossessing them, by force, of their income or wealth. At the same time, knowing human nature as he did, he knew that mere persuasion may not be enough. He therefore conveyed the warning that the alternative to their being amenable to persuasion would be the triumph of forces that would dispossess them by violence. At the same time, he reminded both tenants and workers that their exploitation was possible only because of their failure to recognise their own strength and therefore passively accepting their exploitation. He wanted the poor to use non-violent non-cooperation and civil disobedience for getting the rich to change their attitude and become trustees in the public interest instead of continuing as exploiters. He was prepared to advocate the implementation of ameliorative measures through the legislative channel, give trusteeship a statutory form, and make it a legalised institution. Appeal to the better instincts in the rich, persuasion, education regarding the inevitability of change and the greater unattractiveness of the alternative of change by violence, non-violent non-cooperation by the exploited that would make the exploiter's functioning impossible, and finally legislative action—these were the series of measures that he contemplated as his programme for bringing about the change that he desired in property relations and the use of personal talents in the public interest.

Gandhi also claimed for his socialism of *Sarvodaya* and trusteeship the ability to survive on a self-sustaining and permanent basis which, he held, was not possible in the case of the socialism or communism of the Marxian conception. This was not only because, according to Gandhi, nothing secured by violence could survive on a permanent basis, but also because socialism through violence only destroyed possession but did not destroy possessiveness. Even after existing inequalities of wealth have been removed, the problem of recurring inequalites arising from the varying capacity of talent of individuals will remain. While talent should be fostered, unless it is held in trust to be used in the interests of society, it will again give rise to a privileged class, no matter under what name or garb. Gandhi's vision was prophetic, for the world is now aware of the inequalities that have grown under the Soviet system. In spite of Mao's desperate attempt to destroy an emerging similar trend in China, it is pretty clear that it is only a matter of time before inequalities of income on a large scale will reemerge there as well. Gandhi's doctrine of trusteeship was the only possible answer to the problem of recurring inequalities, assuming, of course that it could be implemented in practice.

The primal force that he envisaged for the accomplishment of his objective was the enlightened individual. "Socialism", he asserted, "begins with the first convert. If there is one such, you can add zeros to the one and the first zero will account for ten and every addition will account for ten times the previous number. If, however, the beginning is a zero, in other words, no one makes the beginning, multiplicity of zeros will also produce zero value. Time and paper occupied in writing zeros will be so much waste".[35] This was entirely in line with his precept and practice, namely, that there must be no distortion between thought and action, and that what one professes one must practise. Replying to the criticism that men of religion, who like him also disdained possession and foreswore private property, had nevertheless been unable to change the social order, he pointed out that godly men, as a rule, had never commended socialism to the masses and did not show enough awareness of the mutual link that bound together both the individual and the society he lived in. He asserted that socialism and even communism were implicit in his own scriptures, but this did not lead to the desired social change, because religious reformers lost faith in the method of conversion of the individual for bringing about change in society. It is this, he said, that led to the birth of the technique of what is known as scientific socialism and added: "I am engaged in solving the same problem that faces scientific socialists".[36] Referring to the western solution that is tarred with the brush of violence, he objects to it because he has seen the wreckage that lies at the end of this road. After conceding that the more thinking set, even in the west today, stand aghast at the abyss towards which their system is heading, Gandhi goes on to say:

> I owe whatever influence I have in the West to my ceaseless endeavour to find a solution which promises an escape from the vicious circle of violence and exploitation. I have been a sympathetic student of the Western social order, and I have discovered that, underlying the fever that fills the soul of the West, there is a restlesss search for Truth. I value that spirit. Let us study our Eastern institutions in that spirit of scientific enquiry and we shall envolve a truer socialism and a truer communism than the world has yet dreamt of. It is surely wrong to presume that Western Socialism or Communism is the last word on the question of mass poverty.[37]

The theory of socialism through trusteeship was the alternative that Gandhi presented to the scientific socialism and communism evolved by the western thinkers. Unfortunately, Gandhi did not have the time to elaborate on his theory of trusteeship. He had been too preoccupied with his experiments in non-violence for the attainment of political freedom and, when freedom came, his life also ended with his final experiment in non-violence for the restoration of communal harmony. Nevertheless, his thoughts on economic change and socialism through trusteeship are found scattered through the years over many pages of his writings and speeches; and there were experiments too, like the indigo dispute in Champaran and the textile strike in Ahmedabad. He has left on record a brief statement[38] that sums up his ideas on trusteeship and given it the shape of a formula or a thesis on the essence of the new social order that he was offering the world as an alternative to the western concept of socialism through violence. The statement is brief enough to be quoted in full:

1. Trusteeship provides a means of transforming the present capitalist order of society into an egalitarian one. It gives no quarter to capitalism, but gives the present owning class a chance of reforming itself. It is based on the faith that human nature is never beyond redemption.
2. It does not recognise any right of private ownership of property, except inasmuch as it may be permitted by society for its own welfare.
3. It does not exclude legislative regulation of the ownership and use of wealth.
4. Thus, under State-regulated trusteeship, an individual will not be free to hold or use his wealth for selfish satisfaction or in disregard of the interest of society.
5. Just as it is proposed to fix a decent minimum living wage, even so a limit should be fixed for the maximum income that could be allowed to any person in society. The difference between such minimum and maximum incomes should be reasonable and equitable and variable from time to time, so much so that the tendency would be towards obliteration of the difference.
6. Under the Gandhian economic order, the character of production will be determined by social necessity and not by personal whim or greed.[39]

This was Gandhiji's reply to the unresolved problem of the new social order. And he derived it from the traditional wisdom of his own country and the unending experiments with truth that constituted his autobiography and made him proclaim that his life was his message. The Gandhian alternative of non-violent change to a just social order based on the principle of trusteeship was his answer to the western panacea of violent change to a just social order based on the coercive use of state machinery.

Gandhi's solution rested on the application of unadulterated non-violence to all aspects of life. Admitting that "it may fail", he asserted nevertheless that "if it does, it will be because of my ignorance of the technique of non-violence".[40] He conceded that while there had been in history many individual votaries of non-violence, society continued to be steeped in violence. There were many noble examples of voluntary poverty and dedicated service, but the social order continued to bristle with exploitation, inequality, and mass poverty. Religion was good, but it was confined to one aspect of life with apparently no similar positive effect on the other aspects of life. The individual stood isolated from society and religion had failed to bring about integration between the two. Gandhi brooded over this paradox and the answer that he arrived at is the key to his philosophy as well as his life activity. "Somehow, or other", he said, "the wrong belief has taken possession of us that *Ahimsa* is pre-eminently a weapon for individuals and its use should, therefore, be to that sphere. In fact, this is not the case. *Ahimsa* is definitely an attribute of society. To convince people of this truth is at once my effort and my experiment".[41] His experiments with *Satyagraha*, non-violence, and non-co-operation, or the use of *Ahimsa* as a social or collective weapon are well known; and have justly given him the high place he occupies in human history as the non-violent revolutionary who brought political freedom to his country. Whether similar success will attend experiments in non-violence for bringing about economic change and achieving a socialism of *Sarvodaya* and trusteeship are still in the womb of the future. The fact is that the experiment has not yet been attempted. And the great exponent of non-violence is no longer there either to conduct the experiment or give his personal guidance to those who may dare to make the attempt.

Few can deny the attractiveness of the Gandhian alternative. The question that many would raise however is whether it will work. Can *Satyagraha* work successfully against domestic vested interests? It is one thing to use *Satyagraha* against a foreigner who lacks local support but would it not be quite a different thing to use it against a fellow citizen who could canvass the support of other citizens who also have vested interests or hope to have them in the future? Instead of being converted, will not the vested interests defend themselves by resort to violence? If they do, will the *Satyagrahis* be able to resist it? Will they get the moral and material support of non-combatants or of public opinion? Will not the power of the State be called in to fight the *Satyagrahi* and protect the vested interests? Should there not be rules to govern the use of *Satyagraha* in order to enable it to retain its moral force; and if so, who will enforce these rules? How will one prevent *Satyagraha* from degenerating into *Duragraha*? Who will maintain and enforce discipline among the *Stayagrahis*? How far can persuasion, education or even example change human nature? What would be the relation between the mandatory power of legislation, the coercive power of State implementation, and the moral authority of non-violence and *Satyagraha*? All these are important questions to which answers are not available, as the world has not had so far any real experience in the use of *Satyagraha* and non-violence for bringing about a revolutionary change in the economic order.

The difficulty about gandhian socialism arises, however, when one seeks to use the principle of trusteeship as the dominant mechanism for the attainment of a socialist society. By the very nature of its moral basis, trusteeship is based upon the voluntary acceptance of its connotation and commitments. Law can spell out the obligations involved only when an individual places his ability or property or both under a trust; but law cannot compel a man to treat either his ability or his property as a trust. The sanction of religion essentially springs from within and can be enforced by a social grouping, not needing either law or force to sustain it, The moment one seeks to use law and force—law always implies, if not an effective use of force, certainly the background of force to secure its implementation—for carrying out the principle of trusteeship and the social use of property or ability, we pass on on to a different plane altogether and get into the realm of socialism—whether scientific or democratic—as it is understood all over the socialist world. There can always be socialist individuals inspired by the ideal of trusteeship and they could well be leaders of socialist parties. But there can be no socialist party based on voluntary trusteeship nor can there be a socialist state built on this principle. This is because human nature is of a mixed character; and its component *gunas* of *sattva, rajas* and *tamas*, are found in varying proportions in human beings. Self-pride, attachment to wealth, and greed for more property are found at least in as much abundance as compassion, non-attachment, and renunciation. From time immemorial, prophets and priests, if not also philosophers and social thinkers, have tried to convert humanity into leading lives of dedication and non-attachment, but the fact remains that, by and large, they have not registered any resounding success. Good people there always are, in every time and clime; and these are the salt of the earth. But these are the exceptions that point the way; they constitute the peaks that gives us the call to climb: But the vast majority of us are earth-bound and selfish and tend to treat both ability and property as instruments for personal aggrandisement. Under the circumstances, any attempt to usher in a socialist society through the mechanism of the principle of trusteeship is not likely to succeed unless it is made a compulsory way of life and such compulsion cannot but rest on force and the formidable apparatus of state machinery which rests ultimately on the sanction of force. This is the dilemma that confronts the gandhian way to socialism through trusteeship. Its uniqueness lies in voluntary acceptance, inner sanction, and non-resort to force; but its practical implementation on a national or global scale involves compulsion, legal sanction and resort to force when necessary. A socialist society is not a collection of religious individuals to whom life and religion are one. It has to be evolved from the bulk of us who are of the earth-earthy and still have inherent and apparently indestructible longings for the more material things of life. That is why we cannot escape legislation, courts, police and the ultimate sanction of socially regulated force, if we are to build up a socialist society in practice.

Nevertheless, Gandhi's ideas are beginning to command increasing attention in a world that is disillusioned by the working of both capitalism and communism and attracted by the possibility that the circle can be squared with economic growth, social justice, full employment, economic and social equality, political democracy, and individual freedoms all forming components of a harmonious new social order. It goes without saying that gandhian ideas have a special appeal in a country like India where he lived and died and which was his field of experiment for the use of *Ahimsa* and *Satyagraha* against foreign rule. It is inevitable therefore that the Indian approach to socialism should take note of the gandhian alternative. Whether it accepts it in toto or not, it can hardly escape drawing on it to the extent that would be of practical import in bringing about the socialist change that is its objective.

REFERENCES

1. India, Ministry of Information and Broadcasting, *Collected Works of Mahatma Gandhi*, Vol. 13, New Delhi : Publications Division, 1964, p. 313.
2. M.K. Gandhi, *Story of my Experiments with Truth*, 2 Vols. Mahadev Desai (ed.), Ahmedabad, Navjivan, 1927-29, p. 220.
3. *Young India*, October 13, 1921.
4. *Harijan*, Vol. 5, No. 35, October 9, 1937.
5. *Young India*, March 17, 1927.
6. M.K. Gandhi, *Hind Swaraj*, Ahmedabad, Navjivan, 1938, pp. 44-45
7. *Harijan*, Vol. 4, No. 29, August 29, 1936, p. 226.
8. *Harijan*, Vol. 6, No. 51, January 28, 1939, p. 438.
9. *Harijan*, May 16, 1936.
10. *Young India*, September 20, 1928.
11. This link-up of the need for manual labour with distaste for the use of machinery has led some critics to dub Gandhi as a mediaeval mystic who was trying to put back the clock of human progress. In fact, in this advocacy of manual labour, even to the length of advocating scaveng ng as an activity that any man could take up, Gandhi was a most modernising agent in the mediaeval Hindu society in which he had been born. The Hindu social system had consigned manual labour to the Sudras who consituted the last of the traditional four Hindu castes; and it had relegated scavenging to be the exclusive occupation of the fifth caste who consequently acquired pollution and became known as untouchables. Not only did this revolt the humanistic conscience of Gandhi but also violated his own conception of the Hindu faith as he derived it from the Hindu scriptures. The fact has to be recognised, therefore, that by advocating manual labour and giving scavenging respectability as an occupation, Gandhi was playing the role of a reformer and a moderniser, who was trying to change the Hindu social structure into some semblance of a modern and more humane society. Manual labour was the *mantra* he found for bringing about this change in the direction of equality among the different castes in the Hindu fold.
12. *Young India*, June 17, 1926.
13. *Harijan*, Nov. 16, 1934
14. *Ibid*. Feb. 12, 1938.
15. *Harijan*, June 22, 1938.
16. Ibid. July 28, 1946.
17. Ibid. Nov., 2, 1934.
18. *Harijan*, Jan. 27, 1940.

19. Ibid. Jan. 28, 1939.
20. Ibid. Jan. 28, 1939.
21. Ibid. June, 1935.
22. Quoted in Pyarelal, *Towards New Horizons*, Allahabad, Navjivan, 1959, pp. 45-46.
23. *Harijan*, Jan. 30, 1937.
24. Address delivered at Guildhall, London, Sept. 23, 1931.
25. Address delivered at Guildhall, London, Sept. 23, 1931.
26. *Harijan*, Oct. 24, 1948.
27. Ibid. March 16, 1947.
28. Ibid, March 31, 1946.
29. M.K. Gandhi, *Constructive Programme : Its Meaning and Place* (Education) Ahmedabad, Navjivan, 1945, p. 20.
30. *Harijan*, Vol. 9, No. 3, Feb. 1, 1942, p. 20.
31. *Harijan*, Vol. 11, No. 24, July 13, 1947, p. 232.
32. *Harijan*, Vol. 11, Nov. 25, July 20, 1947, p. 240.
33. *Young India*, March 26, 1931.
34. Gandhi denied to himself the right to hold any private property, and the only property he left when he died were his spectacles, his pocket watch and his sandals.
38. It is a matter of historical interest that the first draft of this statement was drawn up by an Indian economist steeped in Gandhian values who is still with us, Prof M.L. Dantwala of the Bombay University School of Economics and Sociology. According to my information, the draft was seen by Gandhiji on his silence day. There could therefore be no oral discussion on its contents. But Gandhiji recorded his comments and suggestions for changes on the original draft in his own handwriting. What is quoted here is the version finalised by Gandhiji himself.
39. Quoted in Pyarelal, op. cit., pp. 23-94.
40. *Harijan*, Feb. 20, 1937.
41. *Harijan*, Aug. 25, 1940.

PART TWO

THE INDIAN SOCIALIST EXPERIMENT

The Indian Approach to Socialism

5

SOCIALIST ideas took a long time to come to India. It is true that the words "socialist" and "communist" were used in nineteenth century writings among others of Bankim Chandra Chatterjee, Rabindranath Tagore, Aurobindo Ghosh and Swami Vivekananda, according to Hari Dev Sharma[1] of the Nehru Memorial Museum and Library. The same writer has pointed out that the first Indian reference to Marx was only in 1903 in the *Amrita Bazar Patrika*, while the *Modern Review* published an article on "Socialism and the Social Movement' in 1910 and Har Dayal's article on "Karl Marx—a Modern Rishi" in March 1912. The first biography of Marx in an Indian language was by K. Ramarkrishna Pillai in Malayalam, while an article on Marx appeared in a Gujarati magazine in 1916. It was only after the Russian Revolution in 1917 that socialism made an impact on the Indian mind. And after that, one can trace the emergence on the Indian scene of a Communist Party, several attempts at forming socialist parties, and finally the Congress Socialist Party. The Communist Party came into existence in 1925 and the Congress Socialist Party in 1934.

This belated appearance of socialist doctrines on the political scene was mainly due to the preoccupation of political activists with the securing of national independence and the harnessing together of like-minded forces for the purpose, irrespective of their inequalities in income and wealth or their differing economic objectives or their class basis. Gandhi was the supreme architect and most effective organiser of this national combination, using for this purpose the Indian National Congress and giving it a mass base of the poor and the downtrodden, while, at the same time, winning the support of the professional middle classes, the landowning propertied classes and the well-to-do and wealth-seeking commercial and industrial classes. For obvious reasons, the National Congress, which was spearheading the fight against the British Government for the achievement of Indian independence, could not afford to espouse socialist doctrines with their theme of class conflict that would have divided the national forces and weakened the struggle for national freedom. But this did not make the Congress a capitalist or a bourgeois political party. While its finances came largely from capitalist and pro-capitalist sources, and its organisational skills, political strategy and ideological outpourings from the professional and other middle classes, the strength of the Congress Party lay in the appeal it could make to the poor, illiterate and non-propertied masses in both the rural and the urban areas. And this was because of Gandhi who gave the Congress a mass base and won for it mass support not only because of his pre-eminent spiritual qualities and traditional virtues and the openness to public gaze of his life of simplicity, austerity and sacrifice and a genuineness of conviction and commitment that combined profession with practice, but also because of his concern for mass poverty, his espousal of mass interests and his conspicuous identification with the *Daridra Narayan* which symbolised the masses of his people. His disbelief in the concept of class war, and his countering it by the concept of *Sarvodaya* (or the uplift of all) brought him also the support of the classes, while his doctrine of *Satya* and *Ahimsa* and the strategy of non-violent resistance that he forged from his conviction and his experience in South Africa made him the most formidable opponent that colonialism has had to face in its long history.

In the context of this national imperative and the leadership that Gandhi gave to the national struggle, it was not surprising that communist and socialist parties could not make any significant political headway. Moreover, the sociological and cultural context in which mass awakening was stimulated in the cause of national freedom was not equally conducive to a socialist awakening on the part of the masses. The history and nature of the Indian social structure called for re-examination of the traditional Marxian analysis and a reformulation of the Marxist strategy, especially in the context of a national struggle for political independence. Nor were there present in

India the conditions that prevailed in Europe at the time Marx wrote and influenced Marx in both his analysis of the past and his prognosis for the future.

When Marx wrote, he was confronted by a triumphant capitalism that appeared to deny the possibility of the peaceful establishment of a socialist society. Capitalism was well established in England and had begun to show signs of benevolence domestically, but was indulging in exploitation of colonies abroad and providing material for the later Leninist thesis of imperialism. Capitalism in Europe had started in a somewhat bloody fashion with working class revolts in several countries suppressed by force, and leading to the Marxist cry for uniting the workers of the world, while, within the United States, private enterprise was establishing its dominance in an almost classical Marxist fashion. No wonder that Marx sought in insurrection, force, and proletarian dictatorship the only possible means for the establishment of a socialist society. He tried to provide a scientific basis to his socialist faith and dogma by his materialistic interpretation of history and his prognosis of the inevitable emergence of a socialist society. The background in India, however, was somewhat different. Feudalism in China had retained all its unpleasant features but also worsened sufficiently in the modern period to give the ideological stimulus that was necessary for its violent overthrow. In India, however, feudalism had been "cribbed, cabined, and confined" under British rule; and while retaining its socially and economically reactionary character, nevertheless was shorn of its more unpleasant external features except in some of the smaller princely States.

Even the beginning of industrial capitalism that British rule witnessed in this country was not accompanied by the more unprepossessing features of early industrialisation in the west, as India's British rulers were influenced not only by their developed capitalism but also by their competitive self-interest in giving industrial labour a better deal in India than it had received in their own country during the corresponding period. Above all, there was no significant industrial development in India during British rule and, therefore, there was no chance for the forces of industrial conflict and class hatred to grow in power and prominence as had happened in Europe. At the same time, the forces of nationalism were growing in strength in India and, by the very nature of the case, tending to unite rather than divide the economic classes, the Indian capitalist in embryo being even more interested in the achievement of political independence and its dividends in nationalist economic policy than the worker, while the peasants who were told that there could be no improvement in their economic condition without independence. There was also the further fact of Indian traditional and popular psychology which was non-violent and non-revolutionary and more inclined to tolerance and compromise than was the case in Europe. It was natural, therefore, that the Marxist solution, which was relevant to the contemporary economic and political conditions of his time, did not find acceptance by the vast majority of Indian political workers.

Moreover, Indian Society is unlike most other national societies of the contemporary world in the extent to which it contains sharply varying components and complicated and conflicting factors that prevent the emergence of class differentiation on a purely economic basis. In the Marxcan conception, the basis of socialist revolution was provided by a sharp differentiation and cleavage between the propertied and the non-propertied, the advantaged and disadvantaged, between those who own by inheritance and those who are disinherited by birth. In the context of class differentiation, class consciousness was created and accentuated and it got further stimulated into class hatred. Each unsuccessful revolt of the dispossessed strengthened their class consciousness and class hatred, which then become a focal instrument for social change. This was the conception of the Marxists on which they built their scientific socialism. This was also the actual course of the socialist revolutions that took place in the Soviet Union and in the mainland of China. But Indian society does not easily lend itself to such a phenomenon. Indian society is multi-lingual, multi-religious, multi-caste and multi-regional. Class consciousness of course, is there, but much more than class consciousness is the dominance of linguism, casteism, communalism and regionalism. The result is that class is cut across vertically as well as horizontally by consideration of caste, religion, region and language; and class interests tend to get submerged in communal or linguistic or caste or regional conflicts. These disruptive forces are so powerful that they could overcome even a unifying ideology based on enlightened self-interest, as was illustrated by the abstention from the national struggle of a powerful section of the so-called untouchables and the active hostility of a large section of Indian Muslims which ultimately led to the partition of the country. It should have been obvious therefore that the more limited appeal of a class ideology would not only fail in the face of unifying nationalist ideology but also because of the multiple composition of Indian society that cut across the class concept and favoured group formations on other and more divisive criteria.

The Communist Party of India did not understand the dynamics of the Indian political, social and cultural situation. The founder of the party published a book in 1921 entitled *Gandhi vs Lenin*, which gave a clue to the thinking that dominated the party and its voluntary exclusion from the national mainstream. The party functioned not so much as an Indian national party with an understanding of Indian conditions and Indian issues but as a unit of the world communist movement directed from Moscow. The policy they followed was the one that had been laid down in the Sixth World Congress of the Third International. They accepted the thesis of the reactionary character of the national-reformist character of the Congress Party and the need for unmasking the national reformism of the Indian National Congress and opposing "all the phrases of the Swarajists, Gandhists, etc., about passive resistance with the inconcilable slogan of struggle for the emancipation of the country and the expulsion of the colonialists". Their opposition to the Congress Party enormously diminished the appeal of their ideology to the masses who should have been their principal clientele. Nor was their national credibility enhanced by the role they played during the second World War and the Quit India movement. They thus lost the chance to influence the national struggle into taking a socialist direction which would have given the masses an education in socialist ideas and practices, and made a vital difference to the course of the socialist experiment launched after independence by the leader of the new government of the country.

There were some others who were also Marxists in their thinking and were ideologically close to the Communist Party. But they were also highly patriotic and wanted to go all out to secure political independence for their country. They saw that the Indian National Cogress and the leadership of Gandhi with his hold on the masses were the only effective instruments that could fight the British Government and win national freedom. They did not like the capitalist and bourgeois elements that had such a powerful hold on the Congress; but they believed that it was possible to turn the Congress rank and life in a socialist direction. They were also encouraged by the very important place occupied in the Congress leadership by Jawaharlal Nehru who had openly declared himself as a convinced socialist after his return from Europe in 1927, reiterated his position at the Lahore Congress in 1929 and elaborated his ideas on the subject from the Presidential Chair of the Lucknow session of the Congress in 1936. They also got personal encouragement from him in their efforts to plough the socialist path from within the Congress ranks and looked to him for leadership and decisive action towards a socialist transformation when the time was politically ripe to do so. Hence the formation of the Congress Socialist Party (C.S.P.), which, while working within the Congress in the fight for independence, also functioned and as a left-wing opposition within the Congress to its right wing leadership, and used every opportunity to educate the Congress masses in socialist aims and objectives. There can be no doubt that the C.S.P. played an important role in formulating the Indian approach to socialism with its emphasis on democracy and a non-regimented society.

Gandhi's own position, in spite of his association with nationalistic Indian capitalists, did a great deal to create a favourable climate for the spread of socialist ideas in the country. And he often called himself a socialist. Gandhi's socialism, if one can use this expression in terms of basic values rather than the economic and political framework contained in the modern concept of democratic socialism, stemmed from his belief in God and his interpretation of the Hindu scriptures. According to him, acceptance of the principle of trusteeship by all owners of property, whether material or human, whether of land or capital, or personal ability of various kinds, is in line with the traditions of Indian spiritual teachings from time immemorial.* Personal ability is not a matter of private property even as inherited property is not, while the translation of personal ability or inherited property into acquired property or additions to inherited property are the result of social acceptance and legal sanction. Property is a social concept involving social obligations, while personal ability comes from God and constitutes a sacred trust. To use the principle of trusteeship as the dominant motive force for the Gandhian way to socialism, is, therefore, perfectly in line with Indian traditions.

Jawaharlal Nehru, who was better equipped in economic history and had been influenced both by Marxist teachings and by the Russian Revolution, and might perhaps have become the leader of an Indian Socialist Party on Marxian lines, came under the spell of Gandhi and succeeded him as the national leader, his following including all the economic classes and not only the proletariat. The orthodox Marxist party which might have played a more positive role in the establishment of Marxist socialist ideology among the masses, lost its opportunity through an uncreative and crudely imitative orthodoxy and its failure to perceive the role of the peasantry and the historic role of Gandhi in drawing the peasantry into the national movement. Having failed to appreciate the anti-imperialist role of Gandhi, the Marxist party also failed to link itself with the broad stream of the national movement with its mass power and following. It was, therefore, inevitable that Marx and his concept of scientific socialism failed to strike roots in India as it did in Europe.

At the same time, there was no denying the strong social and economic urges that underlay the Indian national movement and constituted the guiding motive of its top leadership. Gandhi was not an admirer of the modern industrial system and regarded it as an evil that should be fought by prevention rather than cure. At the same time, he was appalled by the poverty of the masses, and by denouncing the urban exploitation of rural India, he gave practical shape to socialist urges, as

* For a detailed discussion of Gandhi's position, the reader is referr e to chapter 4.

the vast bulk of the Indian proletariat was identical with the vast bulk of rural masses. There was perhaps missing in his teachings that sharp economic analysis that one needs for socio-economic change of the dimensions that India required, but recognition of the problem, the need for tackling it, and the building up of a strong emotional urge to do so, all these were in Gandhi's teachings, and they inevitably influenced the public mind in coming to the conclusion that political freedom meant not only the disappearance of foreign rule but also the inauguration of a socio-economic order where the removal of mass poverty would be the major task of political leadership in independent India. Besides this, Gandhi prepared the ground for regulation and limitation of the economic power of the more advantaged classes in the interests of the welfare of the dispossessed masses by his advocacy of simple living, his constant plea for a ceiling on income, and his emphasis on the limitations of private property through the doctrine of trusteeship.

Nehru of course is admittedly the most recognised contributor to the Indian conception of socialism. As indicated earlier, Nehru had been strongly influenced by western socialist ideas and deeply impressed by the Russian Revolution. But the powerful spell that Gandhi laid on him as also his own understanding of the realities of the Indian polity saved him from being a doctrinaire socialist. In fact, he shied away from definitions and felt that a socialistic pattern and socialism were "all exactly the same thing without the slightest difference." He did not like the idea of violent means even for securing a desired objective. He told the Constituent Assembly in 1948[2]: "It is fairly easy to break things up. It is not easy to construct. It is quite possible that in an attempt to change the economic system you may have a period of semi-disaster". He was emphatic on the need to maintain the Indian character of the socialism that the country should adopt. "If the great majority of people in India for some reason or other, become communists, in the sense of thinking that way—that way be good or bad I do not know—but I am quite convinced that it would not be India; then it would be something else. And I do not want that to happen, even though I want India to imbibe modern scientific techniques, scientific theories, economic organisations.

I accept all that to the extent that it is good for India. It is for us to choose. I do not rule out anything, but I do rule out being uprooted from India . . . made into some kind of hot house plant which may look in the hot-house beautiful, but has no roots anywhere in the country".

Nehru's whole approach to socialism was pragmatic. He did not see why he should be asked to define socialism in precise, rigid terms. He asserted.[3]

> It is not a question of theory of communism or socialism. It is a question of hard fact. In India, if we do not ultimately solve the basic problems of our country—the problems of food, clothing, housing and so on, it will not matter whether we call ourselves capitalists, socialists, communists or anything else. If we fail to solve these problems we shall be swept away and somebody else will come in and try to solve them. So ultimately, these major problems of the day are not going to be solved by argument or by way the method that succeeds in delivering the goods. That method need not necessarily be an extreme method belonging to either of these two rival ideologies. It may be something in between.

Nehru, of course, did not agree with Gandhi in his attitude to the modern industrial system. On the contrary, he saw in it the only possible instrument for achieving the economic uplift of the masses, and thought that the remedy for dealing with its evils lay in public ownership, and where this was not feasible, in the regulation and control of private ownership in industry. His basic regard for individual dignity and freedom, his pragmatic approach, his disregard for wholeasale nationalisation and public ownership of the means of production and distribution, and his own understanding of the deeprooted traditional respect of his people for private possession made him reject the concept of a completely state-owned and state operated economy. It was because of this that he advocated the concept of a mixed economy, where the public sector held the commanding heights but left the rest of the arena to private enterprise, subject of course to regulation in the social interest. He also agreed with Gandhi in his basic abhorrence of violence and the promotion of hatred as an instrument of social change;

and he pinned his faith on the capture of state power by the masses through the adoption of a political system, based on democracy, adult franchise and the rule of law. It must be admitted that due allowance was not made by him for the reality of power that accompanies the possession of wealth, even though the individuals concerned may be an infinitely small minority as far as numbers were concerned. Nor did he make enough allowance for the difficulties inevitable in building up mass discipline and determination on an economic basic in a traditional society with a non-revolutionary psychology and divisive urges derived from history. But nevertheless there was no questioning the strength and sincerity of his desire for the establishment of a society that would be egalitarian and conducive to social and economic justice; and his belief in the use of legislative power and the machinery of the state to achieve this purpose constitute an essential part of the background of the Indian approach to a socialist society.

A more thorough approach towards an Indian conception of socialist society than that of either Gandhi or Nehru is that of Vinoba Bhave. Gandhi was not prepared to discard that principle of private ownership even in the case of industrial property. Nehru was not prepared to denounce the principle of private ownership in the case of agricultural land and was content to plead for co-operative farming within the severe limitations of individual ownership. It was Vinoba Bhave who had boldly gone in for the abandonment of the principle of private property in land. "All land belongs to God"—was his constant cry, and in the name of Indian tradition; spirituality and religion, he sought to turn the gandhian principle of trusteeship into an instrument for the setting up of a commonly-owned property an a village basis. He had remarkable success in getting free gifts of land amounting to nearly five million acres, but his achievement fell considerably short of the target of 50 million acres that he had set for himself. There is, however, no denying the fact that his great one-man campaign did shake the country, at least for a short period, and made for some erosion into the concept of private property at its most sensitive point in Indian society, namely, agricultural land. To that extent, his *bhoodan* movement should have been of educational value in preparing the country for a radical change in land and property relations at a later stage. What it did achieve first in Telangana and then elsewhere was the breaking of the monopolistic hold that the communists and their cult of violent dispossession of the propertied were beginning to have on India's agricultural proletariat. To the extent that *bhoodan* succeeded, the prospect of socialism through non-violence and self-sacrifice increased in the countryside. It is true that failure on the organisational side, lack of the needed follow-up action, and the inability of the Nehru Government to exploit the climate created by the *bhoodan* campaign in spite of its professed belief in socialism, all tended to wear away the initial impulses generated by the movement. It is also true that this led to the return of violence and the emergence of the Naxalite movement. All the same, the hard blow that Bhave struck at the institution of private property in land by the weapon of non-violence and moral and spiritual force is an important contribution to the Indian approach to socialism and gives it a flavour and an accent not found in western socialist movements.

In a subsequent chapter, we have dealt with the role of Communist and C.S.P. parties in failing to cash in on Jawaharlal Nehru's admitted socialist inclinations and lend him the active support that may have made a significant difference to the implementation of his socialist ideas. Anyway, when India acquired political independence and Nehru, within a short period thereafter, became the unquestioned leader of the Congress Party and the Government, it was left to him to attempt a socialist transformation of Indian society without the aid of the doctrinaire and dedicated socialists and communists who remained outside, and against the tacit, if not, also overt, opposition from the vested interests who were in such large numbers in his own party and swore allegiance to his leadership. Thus Nehru became a national leader of the government and the people of India, trying to reconcile his national role with his socialist ideas which called for positive action against the vested interests who also constituted an important part of the nation of which he was the leader. Anyway, it was only after independence and the coming of Nehru to dominant power in his country that the Indian approach to socialism began to take concrete shape.

The Constitution that had been adopted in 1950 did contain a strong socialist flavour in its chapter on the Directive Principles and the reference to equality and justice, both economic and social, in its Preamble, in spite of the absence of the Socialist and Communist Parties in the Constituent Assembly; but it was also accompanied by the chapter on Fundamental Rights which was justifiable and created conditions favourable for capitalist development and an inegalitarian society. The Avadi session of the Congress declared itself in favour of adopting a socialist pattern of society as the national goal. Parliament endorsed a similar resolution and the Third Plan spelt out a non-ciassical or middle path strategy for economic and social development in a socialist direction. The Ooty seminar convened by the Congress, at which a few non-party members (the author included) were present discussed the subject and a document indicating some socialist measures was issued at the end of the seminar.* But it was not a comprehensive or integrated programme for socialist development and even the few radical measures it contained failed to get implemented. The socialist pattern of a mixed economy that tried to combine the best from both the capitalist and socialist forms of development, with centralised but largely investment and indicative planning, was adopted for economic development; and socialism became a word of common currency. India was trying to combine parliamentary democracy, fundamental rights of the individual, private property and private enterprise, with a large public sector, planned economic development, social justice and concern for the abolition of mass poverty, in an Indian approach to socialism. The so-called scientific socialism linked to Marxian thinking was rejected and preference given to democratic socialism of the type in vogue in some west European countries. The Indian National Congress accepted the goal of democratic socialism at its Bhubaneshwar session in December 1963, which incidentally, was the last time Nehru attended the plenary session of the Congress. But he had the satisfaction, for what it was worth, of seeing the party, for which he had

*In fact, the author contributed three papers on the socialist aspects of Indian development all of which have been published in the *A.I.C.C Review*.

been working during all his life, officially adopting the goal of socialism, which he had also been espousing throughout his life.

The Bhubaneshwar session of the Indian National Congress amended Article I of its Constitution to read as under :

> The object of the Indian National Congress is the well-being and advancement of the people of India, and the establishment in India, by peaceful and constitutional means, of a socialist state based on parliamentary democracy, in which there is equality of opportunity and a political, economic and social rights, and which aims at world peace and fellowship.

Officially, democratic socialism is now the accepted national goal. The Indian Constitution, adopted in 1950, accepted parliamentary democracy and fundamental rights for the individual as the political system for India while its directive principles of state policy postulated a broad kind of a socialist society as its basic objective. These general principles were given more precise direction when, in December 1954, Parliament adopted "the socialist pattern of society" as the objective of social and economic policy. The Third Five Year Plan document quoted with approval the extracts given below from the Second Plan document, setting out the basic features of what was called the socialist pattern of society.

> . . .Essentially, this means that the basic criterion for determining lines of advance must not be private profit, but social gain, and that the pattern of development and the structure of socio-economic relations should be so planned that they result not only in appreciable increase in national income and employment but also in greater equality in incomes and wealth. . . . . .The benefits of economic development must accrue more and more to the relatively less privileged classes of society, and there should be progressive reduction of the concentration of incomes, wealth and economic power. . . . . .The socialist pattern of society is not to be regarded as some fixed or rigid pattern. It is not rooted in any doctrine or dogma. . . .It is neither necessary nor desirable that the economy should become a

> monolithic type of organisation offering little play for experimentation either as to forms or as to modes of functioning. Nor should expansion of the public sector mean centralization of decision-making and of exercise of authority. . . .The accent of the socialist pattern of society is on the attainment of positive goals, the raising of living standards, the enlargement of opportunities for all, the promotion of enterprise among the disadvantaged classes and the creation of a sense of partnership among all sections of the community. These positive goals provide the criteria for basic decisions. The directive principles of State policy in the Constitution have indicated the approach in broad terms; the socialist pattern of society is a more concretised expression of this approach. Economic policy and institutional changes have to be planned in a manner that would secure economic advance along democratic and egalitarian lines. . .[4]

These extracts appear in the first chapter of the Third Plan, believed to have been personally drafted by Jawaharlal Nehru himself.[5] This chapter also outlines the policies and programmes required for the implementation of the socialist objective for Indian society. These shall be dealt with in the next chapter when discussing the strategy accepted by Government for the transition to socialism.

We may now attempt to difine the Indian approach to socialism. Following the Indian philosophic tradition, it will be apt first define it negatively and then proceed to give some of its positive contents. To being with, most people in this country agree by and large, that the socialism which has been accepted by the country is a socialism that does not believe in the use of violence, while many other countries which talk of socialism do not exclude the use of violence. The Marxian theory presupposes inevitability of the use of violence for the establishment of a socialist society. Quite a large number of people believe that resistance to a socialist society will be such that the vested interests will provoke a class war; and this will lead to a revolution, capture of the state machinery, establishment of a proletarian dictatorship, and the subsequent establishment of a socialist society. We know that ruling out violence for the establishment of a socialist society may mean a certain amount of delay, a certain degree of compromise, a certain measure of accommodation, but nevertheless, we believe this to be important from the long-term point of view. A socialist society established by persuasion and free democratic methods has a greater chance of survival than one established by force.

The second question about the conception of a socialist society is whether the kind of education or persuasion or propaganda or methods of canvassing which will be used for propagating socialism will be based on class hartred or not. On this, there is not really sufficient unanimity of opinion even amongst the socialist parties which are prepared to accept persuasion and non-violence as the instrument for achieving a socialist society. Perhaps one could say, when we are using the language of education and the language of persuasion it is better not to speak of hatred; it is better to use logic and reasoning and exposition of facts for the exposure of wrongs; and such anger as might arise should be a consequence of the exposure of facts rather than the anger which is deliberately created as an instrument of hatred. Gandhi did not hate anybody. He never used the language of hatred. Even when he was sent to jail, he did not blame the man who sent him to jail. But his success was such that, in many ways, we can call him the real father of the liberation movement of Africa and Asia. If India had not become free, African and Asian countries would not have become free. Gandhi had shown the weapon for fighting those who are much more powerful. Thus, our conception of a socialist society is not merely one that abjures the use of violence but also relies fundamentally on education and persuasion and, if necessary, self-suffering for sponsoring the establishment of a socialist order.

The third thing, as far as the Indian conception of a socialist society is concerned, is that it involves socialism with democracy, with human dignity and the creation of opportunities for the development of each individual and not the destruction of the individual. It is not for the merging of the individual in the society. The Indian socialist society wants the development of each individual but requires this development to be such that it leads to the upliftment of the society as well. Therefore, the Indian conception of a socialist society does not involve either dictatorship or any violation of human dignity.

What does a socialist society mean in positive terms in the Indian approach? It means, by and large, that every human being in a society, if he is prepared to work, is able to get work. Those who are not able to work because they are ill, unemployed, handicapped or dumb or blind or old must be ensured a minimum standard of living. In a socialist society, everybody should be able to get a minimum in terms of housing, clothing, food, education and health. But in socialist society, there is no such thing as somebody getting something for nothing. Everybody, who can, should work, but his work must be productive and ensure him and his family a minimum standard of living. People who cannot work for no fault of their own should also get a minimum standard of living. There would therefore be neither poverty nor unemployment in a socialist society.

The second positive attribute is that it must promote equality among its members. It does not necessarily connote an arithmetical equality. A certain amount of inequality is inevitable in any society, whether it is communist or capitalist. What we want in a socialist society is that inequality should be as narrow as possible. There should be some reasonableness in the difference between the top incomes and the bottom incomes. What the difference should be, whether 1-10 or 1-5 or 1-3 is a matter for social judgement. As a corollary of this minimum niequality, there should be equality of opportunity in a socialist society. The system should provide for the discovery and nurturing of talent wherever it exists, irrespective of economic, social or other kinds of backwardness in the parents or groups or environment where it is found. This equality of opportunity is a fundamental condition of a socialist society. The more talent from backward classes and areas gets recognition and support, the more socialist will be that society.

The third positive attribute of the Indian approach is a political democracy that not only functions at the national and the state levels but also at local levels and gives the people a feeling of political participation. Power is expected to be decentralised and its diffusion maintained by an appropriate decentralisation of economic activity. And a mixed economy is postulated with a large public sector and public control of centralised or large scale economic activity in the private sector with prevention of the emergence of monopolistic practices or concentration of economic power. The economy is expected to have the high rate of growth needed for the abolition of poverty together with a built-in mechanism for maintenance and acceleration of the rate of growth in the future for securing secular rise in living standards. Economic effort is expected to be accompanied by increasing self-reliance on domestic resources, both physical and financial and on domestic skills, technology and enterprise. The Indian socialist society is expected to be as good and in fact better than capitalist societies in terms of economic efficiency besides of course being vastly superior in terms of maximisation of employment, equitable distribution of income and special concern for the betterment of the weaker sections of society.

Finally, irrespective of what the income of a person is or the kind of job that he is doing, the Indian approach insists on the maintenance of perfect social equality. Every human being is a person of some worth and deserves equal respect for his individuality. A socialist society must therefore give unqualified support to the social concept of human equality and see that its values, institutions, and practices are such as to lead to the full implementation of this concept is the relations that prevail among its members.

To sum up, the basic values underlying the Indian approach to socialism can be derived from Indian spiritual traditions. Buddhism, Jainism, Vedantic and Bhakti Hinduism, Sikhism, Islam, and Christianity have all contributed to this heritage, not to mention the individual contributions of great Indians in more recent times like Vivekananda, Gandhi, Nehru, Vinoba Bhave and now Jaya Prakash Narain. Indian socialism is rooted in respect for human dignity and human equality. While imposing restrictions on the right to private property even to the extent of abolishing it where necessary in the social interest, it permits private enterprise in economic activity and makes for a mixed economy rather than a completely socialised economy. It abhors violence and class war and pins its faith on non-violence, sacrifice, and dedication to the service of the poor. And as a natural consequence, its implementation is envisaged through parliamentary democracy and the rule of law rather than through a violent revolution or a proletarian dictatorship. Indian socialism therefore is different from Marxist or scientific socialism. While Indian socialism has certainly been influenced by the writings of western socialists, its roots are derived from Indian thinking and adapted to Indian conditions. It is conspicuously Indian in its stress on peaceful change, its belief in the constitutional process, its reliance on parliamentary political democracy, its avoidance of collectivisation of land and its bias for village panchayats, and its preference for decentralisation to the maximum extent possible, of industrial production. Indian socialism is, thus, much more mixed and pragmatic, if not eclectic, than what one found in the west during the early days of its socialist movements. If Indian socialism succeeds in its objective, even to a modest extent, India will have made a significant contribution to the world in socialist theory and practice.

REFERENCES

1. Hari Dev Sharma "The Formation of the Congress Socialist Party", *in* the Paper presented at the Seminar on Aspects of the Economy, Society and Politics in Modern India 1900-1950, (Dec. 15-18, 1980,) New Delhi.
2. *Constituent Assembly debates*, 1948.
3. V.K. R.V. Rao, *The Nehru Legacy*, Bombay, Popular Prakashan, 1971, p. 60.
4. Second Five Year Plan, Govt. of India, The Planning Commission, pp. 22-24.
5. The Third Plan draft, which had been published earlier did not contain any reference to socialism. Writing in (V.K.R.V. Rao, Ideology of Third Plan, *Yojana*, Vol. 4, No. 14, July 24, 1960, p. 4) on this document the author drew pointed attention to this omission and stated that the call for public cooperation in implementing the plan sounded in this context like a "call to battle without a battle cry"; and his remarks were quoted with approval in the Lok Sabha by a leading member of the Opposition, Prof. Hiren Mukherjee. He also had it on good authority that what he wrote had something to do with Jawaharlal Nehru's intervention in revising the draft and personally writing the first chapter, spelling out in detail the history of the socialist background of Indian planning and dealing concretely with the policies, programmes and strategy of socialist development for India.

The Indian Experiment in Socialist Transformation

6

IN THE light of what has been described as the Indian approach to socialism, there was perhaps no alternative to the adoption of a mixed economy for bringing about a democratic socialist society in India.

When India started its socialist experiment, the Soviet Union had already established a socialist society but this had been preceded by a violent revolution, a proletarian dictatorship of the state, abolition of private property and a one-party Communist party rule quite different from the parliamentary democracy to which India had committed itself. The Soviet example was obviously out of the question in the Indian context except for its use of planning for economic development. Some parliamentary democracies in the West had brought about or were trying to bring about a socialist pattern in their societies, which did not involve the abolition of private property in all means of production, and mainly meant the creation of a welfare state rather than a socialist society. They were able to do so, because this had been preceded by an industrial revolution, and development and accumulation through a capitalist exploitation made easy by the absence of a parliamentary democracy in their countries of the kind with which we are now familiar and which we have adopted now in our own country. For us in India, however, economic development was yet to take place, accumulation had still to be undertaken, and economic activity had to be organised and economic growth had to be accelerated in the context of a working parliamentary democracy based on adult franchise, civil liberties, electoral pressures, and a multi-party system that could appeal to and mobilise the have-nots to pressure the government to function in their favour. This meant that the Indian socialist experiment had to rely for economic development less on the role of private capital with its profit motive and more on public and social capital mobilised by government and the community. In other words, economic development had to be based more on mobilising mass participation in both production and accumulation than on private capitalist enterprise and accumulation. The use of a mixed economy was therefore a compromise solution which sought to bring about economic development but with a socialist accent, giving room to both a public and private sector, and a state policy aimed at promoting economic growth with social justice.

The Indian strategy for socialist development and the transition to a socialist society was the result of Nehru's thinking. The Nehruvian concept of a mixed economy as the Indian strategy for socialist development was based on the realities of the Indian situation, his regard for the individual's dignity and freedom, and the influence of Gandhi on his political and social thinking. Nehru of course never spelt out his ultimate picture of Indian socialist society. His attitude was pragmatic and practical and, like Gandhi, he believed in one step at a time. He recognised that there could be no change in a socialist direction in the Indian countryside without land reforms, dispossession of ownership without cultivation, linking of cultivation with ownership, ceiling on land holdings and distribution of the resultant surplus land to the landless. Visualising the rural structure essentially as one of peasant proprietorship, he sought to introduce the socialist principle therein by propagating the doctrine of cooperative cultivation or even lesser form of cooperative in one or more of agricultural practices. While giving a large place to the private sector in industry, he gave a larger place to the public sector to which he sought to give the commanding heights in the economy by concentrating it on capital and basic goods while leaving consumer goods out of its purview. Influenced to some extent by the Soviet model as a successful technique for economic growth, he laid emphasis on heavy industries as a priority item of investment and capital accumulation. There was no reference in his programme either to nationalisation of banking or of wholesale trade, while the financing institutions that were established under the mixed economy in the national sector were primarily intended to meet the requirements of private large scale industry, while those established in the States sectors were for meeting the requirements of medium and small scale industries in the private sector. The private sector investments were sought to be controlled by a licensing system for capital issues, and a licensing system for new manufacturing units and their scheduled capacities, which determined their quotas of import inputs, import and export control, and foreign exchange control. Thus Nehru's conception of mixed economy aimed at a commanding public sector and a regulated private sector, with finance and trade largely left in private hands. This was presented by Nehru as the strategy for ushering in a society that would both be industrially developed and socialistic in character. It was also presented as a non-classical or a middle-path strategy of economic and social development.

The strategy was spelt out in more detail in the first chapter of the Third Plan which, as stated earlier, is believed to be Nehru's personal draft. On the policy side it was stated :

(1) Above all a socialist economy must be efficient, progressive in its approach to science and technology, and capable of growing steadily to a level at which the well-being of the mass of the population can be secured. In an underdeveloped country, a high rate of economic progress and the development of a large public sector and a cooperative sector are among the principal means for effecting the transition towards socialism.

(2) In the second place, a socialist economy should ensure equality of opportunity to every citizen. As a first step, it should provide for the basic necessities, in particular for food, work, opportunity for education, reasonable conditions of housing, and a minimum level of income which, in the given circumstances, will ensure tolerable living standards.

(3) In the third place, through the public policies it pursues, a socialist economy should not only reduce economic and social disparities which already exist, but must also ensure rapid expansion of the economy but without concentration of economic power and growth of monopoly.

(4) Finally, a socialist development on the basis of democracy and socialism is bound to place the greatest stress on social values and incentives and on developing a sense of common interest and obligation among all sections of the community.[1]

Implied in these policies are programmes for making a significant use of the public and cooperative sectors for securing a high rate of economic growth, use of progressive science and technology, having a product-mix of domestic output that will give a national minimum of mass consumption goods, use of a production technology that will maximise employment, reduction of economic and social disparities, prevention of concerned of economic power through appropriate public policy, and building up of social values and incentives.

Among the programmes mentioned for the rural areas were :

(1) land reforms and reform of the agrarian system;
(2) increase in agricultural production and productivity;
(3) fuller utilisation of available manpower and other resources;
(4) development of local initiative and responsibility and cooperative self-help;
(5) creation of conditions for the growth of progressive rural cooperative economy with a diversified occupational structure in which the weaker sections are brought speedily to the level of the rest; and
(6) development of a cooperative agro-industrial economy in the Rural areas.

In regard to industry were mentioned :

(1) speeding up of industrial development through planned development;
(2) development of heavy industries and machine making industries;
(3) growth of the public sector both absolutely and at a faster rate than the private sector;

(4) giving the private sector a large area in which to develop and expand but within the framework of national planning and an understanding of its obligations to the community as a whole;
(5) giving village and small scale industries a crucial role in the development of the national economy;
(6) spreading the benefits of industrialisation evenly between different parts of the country; and
(7) giving full scope, within the framework of a national planning, to new entrepreneurs, to medium and small scale enterprises, and to cooperative organisations.

In respect of organisation of economic activity, the stress is on the public and cooperative sectors, and on new entrants and small scale units in the private sector. Thus :

(1) The rapid expansion of the public sector is intended to remove certain basic deficiencies in the economic structure and at the same time reduce the scope for accumulation of wealth and large incomes in private hands.
(2) To the greatest possible extent feasible, construction and supply functions for state undertakings should be entrusted to public and cooperative agencies.
(3) With the increasing share of the public sector, the state will be in a stronger position to determine the character and functioning of the economy as a whole.
(4) Licensing of new industrial units and expansion of existing units should be such as to prevent the growth of large business and facilitate the entry of new firms, medium enterprises and cooperative organisations.

As regards reducing disparities in incomes, the following programmes were envisaged :

(1) Land reforms with its abolition of intermediary rights, security and rent reduction for tenants and ceiling on agricultural holdings;
(2) reduction in dependence on land and diversification of the economic structure of the rural areas through

extension of industry and development of social services on an adequate scale;

(3) an agricultural price policy which is both fair to the urban consumer and fully safeguards the farmer's interest;

(4) reducing the spread between higher and lower incomes and raising the level of the minimum;

(5) state appropriation of a due share of capital gains, speculative profits and the like; and

(6) full implementation of tax obligations, reduction of tax avoidance to the maximum and severe treatment for tax evasion.

Finally, the strategy laid stress on the need for urgency and quickening the pace in implementing the programme, adopting more critical tests for evaluation, and more determined implementation of accepted policies in all spheres of public administration.

Nehru was Prime Minister of India right from the onset of Independence up to his death in May 1974. The strategy he adopted did bring in a measure of economic growth. During the first plan period, the annual rate of growth was 3.4 per cent, during the second plan period 4 per cent, and in the first four years of the third plan period 4.2 per cent. In aggregate terms India's national income increased by about 69 per cent from Rs. 9850 crores to Rs.16630 crores at 1960-61 prices between 1950-51 to 1964-65 at a compound rate of 3.8 percent a year.[2]

Of course it was less than what was sought but it did mark a significant rate of progress from the near stagnation of the pre-Independence period when national income was growing at the rate of barely one per cent a year. But the rapid growth of population during the period largely nullified the dividends of this growth, per capita income in real terms in creasing during this period by only 28 per cent or at an annual average of about 1.8 per cent. While the index of agricultural production increased during this period of fourteen years by 65 per cent that of industrial production increased by 146 per cent. Public sector investment in industry grew much faster than private investment and the share of the public sector in the reproducible tangible wealth of the country increased from about 15 per cent in

1950-51 to 35 per cent in 1965-66. The country also saw substantial increase in the production of capital goods, intermediate goods and machinery. There was also a significant growth in social capital measured by the increase in the number of students in educational institutions in arts, science, commerce, engineering, medicine and agriculture, and in hospital beds and primary health centres.

While these production efforts did yield some significant results in terms of economic development, they did not succeed in bringing about the socialist transformation which was also a part of his objective. Economic growth was not up to expectations, reduction in economic disparities was negligible, improvement in the level of living standards of the masses was also negligible, the national product-mix was not weighted in favour of mass consumption goods, big cities continued to grow while rural areas did not record significant development, equalisation of opportunities did not extend to the masses, unemployment increased, and so did poverty both in rural and in urban areas. On the whole, what emerged was a dual society in which a small minority of the population enjoyed a good standard of living, urban amenities, a product-mix that catered to their consumption demand, and economic power, and political influence bordering on control; the vast majority on the other hand continued to remain poor with low consumption standards, a high level of unemployment, low level of economic and other opportunities, only a few of the amenities enjoyed by the elite, and neither participation nor control over the power structure, both political and economic. The growth of the public sector did but little to help the masses; while that of the private sector helped to widen disparities of income and increase the concentration of economic power. Tax evasion continued, controls encouraged corruption instead of regulation and there was a decline in social values. The society that emerged in India by the time Nehru left the scene was certainly not the one which he planned. Some of the defects noticed in the economic programme adopted by Nehru were rectified by Indira Gandhi when she became Prime Minister. Thus the 14 major units of the commercial banking system were nationalised and some guidelines for their working embodied in the legislation which brought about nationalisation. The coal industry was also nationalised. The company law was amended and a commission set up to deal with monopolistic practices in industry. An attempt was made to make land reforms more effective, reduce ceiling, and speed up implementation. A special machinery was set up to help the weaker sections in the rural areas such as small farmers, marginal farmers and agricultural labourers. Industrial licensing rules and other controls were liberalised, and stern action was initiated against tax-evaders, smugglers and blackmarketeers. Effective steps were taken to control the inflation that had burst on the country during her period and there was a big rise in foreign trade and a spectacular rise in both foreign exchange holdings and domestic food stocks held by government. The Twenty Point Programme which she initiated, while not deserving all the lyrical and sycophantic encomiums heaped upon it, did include some useful measures for weakening the hold of the rural elite on the rural power structure and giving sustainable relief to the weaker sections in the rural areas.

While these measures marked some advance over the Nehru period in terms of combining social justice with economic development, it did not bring about the desired rise in the rate of economic growth. The annual average rate of growth during these 8 years of Mrs Gandhi's prime ministership was 4.05 per cent in real national income and 1.36 per cent in per capita income, while during the 14 years of Nehru's prime ministership, the corresponding figures were higher being 5 per cent in national income and 2 per cent in per capita income. However, Mrs Gandhi's period also showed a significant break-through in Indian agriculture because of the successful green revolution in some parts of the country and gave the nation real confidence that it could now conquer its food problem. However, the fact remains that there was no significant improvement either in employment or the incidence of poverty or in the disparity of income and wealth. At the same time, there seemed to emerge a tendency to go back on socialist premises and give larger tax concessions and relief from control to revive the luxury goods market and stimulate the private sector in the belief that it may step up the rate of economic growth.

The most serious departure from the socialist strategy however was the drastic abridgement of a major premise of democratic socialism namely, parliamentary democracy, civil freedoms and the protective rule of the judiciary. Though there was a fall in smuggling and black money, corruption increased, many excesses were committed under the family planning programme, bureaucratic power grew and many thousands of people were imprisoned. National political life came to a standstill and the country was gripped by a numbing fear-psychosis. Socialism and economic development slipped into the background in the public mind which now became more concerned with the political problem of restoration of of parliamentary democracy and individual freedoms. And Mrs Gandhi's long rule of 11 years as Prime Minister ended when the Janata Party won the general elections in 1977 and practically wiped out the Congress party from the north-west, north-east and central India.

The party which came to power in 1977 had no past as a political party—in fact it came into existence only on the eve of the elections—nor did it have any cohesion or a single and integrated ideology, mainly because of its enormously disparate interest structure. It is true that at its first national convention, the newly formed Janata Party declared its objectives in ideological terms as under:

> Building up a democratic, secular and socialist state in India by gandhian principles, drawing inspiration from our rich heritage and noble traditions of our struggle for national independence and individual liberty.

The Janata Party's object also included "decentralisation of economic and political power." Socialism of some kind thus continued as a link between the old and new regimes. The party was however wholly disunited, and much of its time was in open and spent unseemly quarrels among its top leaders, and inquiring into the faults of commissions and omissions of the previous government. The party's major contribution was the restoration of individual freedom and judicial independence to its pre-emergency levels; but in advancing the country towards a socialist society, its record was most uninspiring. For the first time in post-independent India's political history, the central government presented an unseemly and undignified spectacle that brought about deep popular disillusion. Nor did the conduct of the new opposition led by Mrs Gandhi add any dignity to the political scenario. The fall of the Janata Government and its replacement by a Charan Singh-Chavan coalition were both illustrations of the depths to which Indian politics had descended within less than three decades after the achievement of independence. The politics of the leftist parties, evidently based on their conception of what was expedient, which led to their changing alliances with other political parties, certainly did not add to the prestige of the socialist ideology among the people. It was not surprising therefore that when the mid-term elections came, the people threw out the ineffective and unprincipled newcomers to political power and returned their allegiance to the person whom they had known not only as a decisive leader but also as one who, they felt, was genuinely wedded to the interests of the poor and disinherited sections of Indian society. And Mrs Gandhi resumed her position as Prime Minister after an interval of less than three years from her previous sway of eleven years. At the time of writing, and with the complete disarray among the quarrelling and disunited opposition parties, it appears more than probable that Mrs Gandhi will continue to be in power for a foreseeable period.

The thirty year Indian experiment in socialist planning has thus ended without effecting the socialist transformation dreamed of by Nehru in spite of the economic development which has taken place, because of the deficiencies, distortions, disparities and class alignments which accompanied it. But the country has not given up its socialist aspirations nor have Indian political parties given up the socialist goal. In fact the socialist objective is now a part of the Preamble to the Indian Constitution. The future is still to unfold itself on the social and economic fronts and the country has yet to know how Mrs Gandhi's new government proposes to move towards a socialist transformation of Indian society against the background of the uneven and distorted development which has taken place during the last thirty years. There is however no doubt that continuity will be sought to be maintained as far as the Indian approach to socialism is concerned. Chapters 3 and 5 of this volume should therefore become relevant material in this context.

Democracy has not given India a socialist society under Nehru's regime. Nor had its abridgement under his daughter's rule. But democracy and general elections are now here to stay, as far as India is concerned. It is now for the country to find a workable way towards the desired socialist transformation within the constraints or otherwise of a parliamentary democracy, make such changes in the system of government as will, while promoting socialist transformation, deny the possibilities of a political or economic or social dictatorship, and ensure the maintenance of democracy and the retention of civil freedoms, and an independent judiciary.

REFERENCES

1. Third Five Year Plan, Govt. of India, The Planning Commission, pp. 9-10.
2. Draft outline of Fourth Five Year Plan, August, 1966.

Failure of the Socialist Experiment 7

INDIA has now had more than thirty years of political independence, and nearly thirty years of parliamentary democracy and a planned economy. The avowed objective has been the building up of a socialist society in the light of the general approach outlined in chapter 5 with a functioning political democracy, a mixed economy geared to a socialist ideology, a labour intensive and decentralised economy, maximisation of employment, abolition of poverty, self-reliance and rapid economic development with social justice, with a built-in mechanism for continuing and accelerating economic growth. These have been the objectives placed before the country by the Congress Party during the last thirty years. And the Congress Party has been in control of the Central Government for the bulk of these thirty years and also of most of the state governments for most of the time. Presumably therefore the country ought to have made some significant progress in the achievement of the avowed objectives. And yet the sad fact remains that in spite of considerable development and increase in national output, we have failed to make any significant advance either in the rate of economic growth or in social justice or in reducing unemployment or abolishing poverty or in bringing about a decentralised economy. It is therefore worthwhile making a brief analysis of our experience in attempting to accelerate economic growth with social justice and laying the foundations of a democratic socialist society in India. Failure facilitates diagnosis: and diagnosis should enable the formulation of workable prescriptions.

To begin with, poverty has not disappeared from the country. Of course, it is not reasonable to expect the total disappearance of poverty within such a short period when it involves so many hundreds of millions and such a vast country like India. But one does expect some visible and fairly substantial progress to be made in this direction over a period as long as three decades. In actual fact, however, to the extent to which National Sample Survey results and ad hoc research by social scientists can be trusted as reliable indicators of change, it appears that there has actually been an increase in the number of people below the poverty line in India; and this is especially so during the last fifteen years. How is this possible in the light of the undoubted progress that the country has made in increasing agricultural output, increasing and diversifying industrial production, expanding education and technical and non-technical skills in the country, increasing public expenditure and public investment, increasing the volume of foreign trade, enlarging foreign exchange receipts, and obtaining many thousands of crores of foreign aid? This paradoxical situation can only be explained by the hypothesis that there was something wrong with the policy frame behind the development, and the technology and administration of its implementation. What has been created is an illusion of moving towards the nationally committed goals of socialist development. And it is this illusion which has prevented the changes in policies, programmes and implementations, that are needed actually to move towards the accepted goals of development.

One such illusion has been the spectacular economic growth in absolute, though not in percentage, terms evidenced by the increase in domestic output and particularly by the growth of industrial production and income from the tertiary sector. Behind this, for example, was the fact that non-durable consumer goods output had a weight of only 31.57 per cent in the industrial index and recorded a growth of 90.30 per cent during the period 1961 to 1978 as against a growth of 167.22 per cent in the general index of industrial production. On the other hand, capital goods industries recorded a rise of 252.17 per cent, durable consumer goods of 268.76 per cent, basic industries of 360.04 per cent, and of intermediate industries 115.68 per cent. Agricultural output as a whole increased by 56.38 per cent, cereals as a group rising by 66. 27 per cent but with only 55.27 per cent rise in rice which accounts for 60 per cent of cereal consumption and 33.8 per cent rise in jowar and 35.32

per cent rise in bajra, which constitute the poor man's cereal, and an actual fall of 7.57 per cent in pulses which is the poor man's only source of proteins. Groundnut, a major source of edible oil, increased by only 29.17 per cent.

Another way of looking at the reality behind India's economic development is to see the growth which has taken place at constant prices in terms of sectoral outputs. Thus during the period 1960-61 and 1978-79, output of the primary sector increased in real terms from Rs. 6831 crores to Rs. 10028 crores or by 46.8 per cent, whereas that from the secondary sector increased from Rs. 2683 crores to Rs. 6669 crores or by 148.57 per cent and of the tertiary sector from Rs. 3871 crores to Rs. 9453 crores or by 147.40 per cent. This should be viewed against the background of the distribution of the working population according to the 1981 census among these three sectors. Thus the agricultural sector accounted for 146.8 millions or 66.7 per cent of the total working force, and the non-agricultural sector for 73.3 millions or 33.3 per cent. Another way of looking at the reality behind Indian economic growth is to look at the extent of rise in the real wages of industrial workers. While the index of money earnings of factory workers increased from 100 in 1961 to 192 in 1972 or doubled, the index of real earnings according to official statistics rose only to 103 or practically remained constant during the period. The cost of living index of agricultural labourers rose during 1961 to 1972 from 100 to 225 but there was no corresponding increase in their money earnings with the result that their real earnings actually registered a decline. The number of people below the poverty line irrespective of the definition given to poverty in constant money terms, rose significantly during the period and the poor remained in more or less constant proportion of the population round about 50 per cent. Certainly one cannot deduce from these figures that economic growth was being accompained by social justice or that the dividends from development were being distributed in an equitable manner either between the rural and urban areas or between the masses and the classes.

Even in regard to the increase that has taken place in agricultural production and the benefits derived from the so-called green revoution, it must be remembered that the distributive effects are primarily determined by the incidence of the ownership of land and other assets in the rural areas. That this distribution was far from being equitable and was therefore bound to affect the equitable character of the benefits of growth in the rural areas is clear from the following table compiled from official sources.

Thus, 50.6 per cent of the holdings accounted for only 9 per cent of the area, while 3.9 per cent of the holdings accounted for 30.9 per cent of the area. As regards the ownership of all assets in rural areas including land, as Reserve Bank Survey for 1971-72 showed that more than one-third of the total number of rural households owned assets valued at less than Rs. 2500 each, which included one-fifth of the total number of cultivators, nine-tenths of the agricultural labourers, more than seven-tenths of the artisans, and about two-thirds of "other" non-cultivators. The average value of assets per thousand in this group worked out to Rs 987 of which, excluding land and buildings, durable household assets accounted for Rs. 137 livestock for Rs. 122, implements and machinery for Rs. 28 and financial assets for Rs. 20.

Another aspect of the reality behind the country's economic growth can be seen from the impact it has had on employment in the organised sector. During the period 1961 to 1977, estimated employment in the public and private sector increased from 11.0 million to 20.7 million or by 9.7 million. During the same period, the number of applicants on the live register of the Employment Exchanges increased from 1.8 million to 10.9 million or by 9.1 millions. In other words, persons who were still seeking employment in the public and private sectors increased by a number not significantly below that of the persons who actually got employment. Of the 10.9 millions on the live register of applicants in 1977, 5.1 million 46.8 or per cent were educated persons with academic qualifications of matriculation and above; and their number had reached this level from 0.6 million in 1961, recording an increase of 4.5 million during the period. As regards rural unemployment and underemployment, while no detailed data is available, the dimensions of the problem have been indicated by an official committee for 1970 as 7.7 million of wholly unemployed, and 32 million of underemployed of whom 23.5 million were estimated to have less than 24 hours of work per week and 8.5 million less than 14 hours of work per week.

TABLE **1** : **The size distribution of India's 70.5 million agricultural holdings in 1970-71 according to the agricultural census**

Category of holdings.	Size group	Number (888)	Per-cent	Area (000 hect-ares)	Per-cent
Marginal	Less than 1 hectare	35,682	50.6	14,545	9.0
Small	1.0 to 2.0 hectares	13,432	19.0	19,282	11.9
Semi-medium	2.0 to 4.0 hectares	10,681	15.2	29,999	18,5
Medium	4.0 to 10.0 hectares	7,932	11.3	48,234	29.7
Large	10.0 hecta-res & above	2,766	3.9	50,064	30.9
All catego-ries		70,493	100.0	162,124	100.0

A side-light on the employment problem can be obtained from the official Annual Survey of Industries which showed that while the fixed capital (machinery and equipment) used in industry rose from Rs. 11342 million in 1959 to Rs. 83670 million in 1970, or by 638 per cent, the number of persons employed rose from 28.7 lakhs to 42.6 lakhs or by only 48 per cent. The fixed capital used per worker increased from Rs. 3952 to Rs. 19655 or by nearly five times during this period. If we take the fixed capital used per newly employed worker during this period, it was as much as 13 times the amount employed per worker at the beginning, being Rs. 52147 as compared to Rs. 3952 in 1959.

For promoting equity in distribution, and encouraging the growth of savings, economic development has to be largely non-inflationary and the price level should be restraining from having more than a marginal rise. This has however not been the case with India's economic growth, especially during the last fifteen years. Thus, while national income increased from

Rs. 13335 crores in 1960-61 to Rs. 81429 crores in 1978-79, or by 511 per cent at current prices, the increase in real national income was only 96 per cent income at 1960-61 prices being only Rs. 26150 crores in 1978-79. Apart from the undesirable social and economic consequences of such an inflationary rise of money incomes, the growth in real income achieved during the period certainly cannot be called satisfactory especially for a developing country with a planned economy. During the same period, per capita national income at constant prices rose only by 29.5 per cent, because of the increase in population by 144 million. Obviously the developmental effort was not commensurate with the avowed growth objective; and even such results as were obtained were largely nullified by the growth in population.

The mixed economy basis in the Indian strategy for socialist development visualised for the public sector, what were called the "commanding heights", and for the private sector socially determined objectives which were to be implemented by regulation, control, and incentives. The socially determined objectives included maximisation of employment, dispersal and decentralisation of economic activity, development of backward regions, and prevention of monopolies, monopolistic practices, and centralisation of economic power. In actual fact this strategy failed in securing its objective. While the public sector undoubtedly grew at a very rapid pace during this period it did not show any evidence of commanding heights in the sense of either commanding the economy or private sector enterprise nor did it give an adequate return on the capital invested in it. As far as the private sector was concerned, while there was some noticeable growth in what is called the small industries sector, big enterprises grew bigger and, to a large extent, on the basis of funds provided by loan finance from either the public sector or commercial banks and with the help of the infrastructural facilities provided by government at considerable public expense. There was no significant flow of private capital or enterprise to the backward regions. And the controls and regulations established to direct the private sector in socially desired channels and prevent the emergence of monopolies and concentration of economic power failed in their purpose. In fact, industrial licences, import licences, foreign exchange licences and the rest helped to bring about the very results which were not desired and also led to corruption, black money, and abnormal profits. Though a Monopolies and Restricted Trade Practices Commission has been set up and legislation has been passed and company law amended, concentration of economic power continues to grow; and a whole climate of bribery and corruption has emerged which has affected both the controllers and the controlled. How to control the private sector without its resulting corruption and how to control it effectively has become a big problem which has been enhanced by the way in which our parliamentary democracy has been functioning in recent years.

Parliamentary democracy also has not played the role expected of it in promoting economic growth with social justice and without inflation. There has been an undue insistence on rights without any regard for duties, sectional and group interests asserting themselves without any regard for the social interest and taking resort to agitational methods creating a climate of violence, all leading to a situation adversely affecting economic growth without at the same time producing any effective results by way of social justice. Thus the Indian strategy has failed to achieve its objective of taking the country in the direction of a democratic socialist society in spite of the considerable economic growth it was able to achieve.

This paradoxical situation can only be explained by the hypothesis that there was either something wrong with the policy frame behind the development or with regard to its programmes or with the technology and administration of its implementation. Perhaps the root of the problem lay in Nehru's neglect of the politics of economic development under a mixed economy and its relation to both the political and economic power structure in the context of an attempt at socialist transformation. There was more than a grain of truth in what Professor Oscar Langes[1] distinguished Polish Marxist and economist, wrote when asked to sum up the relevance of the Russian and East European models for developing countries like India:

It can be stated as a general principle that successful planning for economic development must imply the abolition—or at least neutralisation—of such concentration of economic power as would block the realisation of the plan. What this involves in terms of concrete measures will vary with particular historical cirumstances of each country and may even vary at different stages of a country's planning experience. The concrete solution will depend on how such private concentration of economic power align themselves with the general objectives of national economic planning. Their alignment, in turn, may depend on the extent to which the Government charged with the task of realisation of a national plan of economic development is able to marshal the support of the people and of their organisations. Beyond this no general statement can be made. The particular application to a country like India must be undertaken by persons more competent than the writer of these lines.

Nehru's failure to achieve economic growth in the direction of a socialist transformation does not mean that his basic policy of using a mixed economy for the purpose was wrong. A mixed economy depends for its success on the crucial factor of how state intervention is used to regulate its working. And there are a host of differences between an injudicious, partial and ineffective state intervention and a judicious, strategic and effective intervention by the state and other social agencies. A mixture of the genuine socialistic and of the progressive capitalist elements, both of which work for national self-reliance and abolition of mass poverty, could be called a right mix for the mixed economy. But it becomes a wrong mix, if it means a combination of feudal and mercantilist-cum-usurious capitalist elements on the one hand and parasitic and inefficient state-capitalist elements on the other. Mere extension of state ownership or even the introduction of a full-fledged state owned economy does not ensure the automatic realisation of a socialist society; in fact, in the absence of certain other conditions, it could easily degenerate into a vast bureaucratic empire, a paradise for the power-loving politicians, bureaucrats and technocrats. Past experience has shown that institutions can serve socialist aims only if there exists a high level of social consciounsness and organisation in every section of society and especially among the weaker sections who have the major stake in socialism. In order to lead to socialist transformation, these institutions need to be manned by cadres dedicated to the socialist cause and possessing organisational ability and technical skill of a high order. In the absence of these conditions, the state may have all the commanding heights in the economy, but they may be used not for strengthening socialism but for strengthening private economic or bureaucratic or sectional working class power. The statute book may contain all the laws necessary to punish those who try to obstruct the transition to socialism, but the state may not be able to or even willing to use this coercive apparatus and be made to function as a 'soft-State' of Myrdalian[2] description. Even in the Soviet Union, non-institutional factors made a tremendous difference to the quality of functioning of Soviet economic institutions. A mixed economy therefore may function quite differently according to the extent it enables the weaker sections to get organised and the use it makes of non-institutional factors to strengthen its socialist thrust.

A demarcation can be made between two alternative patterns of mixed economy. In what may be called Type A, the state agencies and the public sector provide external economies, infrastructural facilities, generation of technical skills, loan finances, tax concessions, export inducements and a whole host of other incentives to the private sector and enable it to grow at a fast pace. In doing so, they take no account of the social or kinship or ideological elements in those who are thus assisted to grow in the private sector, do not ensure an equitable distribution of the dividends from such growth or take account of its effect on inequality of incomes and wealth or offer any effective opposition to the concentration of economic power in private hands.[3] In effect, the public sector, far from operating a position of commanding heights over the private sector, becomes an adjunct to the private sector or is ineffective in its attempt to control or regulate its activities. At the same time the public sector is not able to obtain a position of moral superiority either because of its operational inefficiency largely from self-created causes. Under Type A of mixed economy, the private sector thus acquires a dominant influence in economic terms and indirectly also in political terms by the use it makes of its economic power in the context of a parliamentary democracy and expensive elections. In the other type of mixed economy, which may be called Type B, the state uses the Public Sector including state power as commanding heights to determine the main directions of the country's economic development, not only by appropriate action in its own area but also by effectively influencing the investment pattern in the private sector, its ownership and operation, and its product-mix in terms of basic consumption goods and luxury goods. It takes effective steps to prevent concentration of economic power in private hands and sees to it that the economic power of the private sector gets widely dispersed and decentralised so that it cannot acquire any direct or indirect political influence of an anti-socialist character. It does not confine its production activities only to infrastructure or capital goods, but also extends it to consumer goods so that the commanding heights also become lucrative heights, ensuring thereby an acceleration in the tempo of capital formation and resource mobilisation. It also acquires effective control over such key sectors of the private sector as stock exchanges, markets in land and real estate, trading in gold and jewellery, banking and wholesale trade in crucial commodities. It also prevents private capitalist interests from controlling the press and other mass media. For its own part, it sets an example in the operational efficiency, profitability and viable pricing policy in the economic activities it directly undertakes through its public enterprises. Under Type B, a mixed economy gives the public sector a truly commanding position in the economy, though a vast majority of the work force may continue to be engaged in or employed by the private sector. The Indian experiment in mixed economy tended to conform to Type A rather than Type B. Hence its failure to bring about the desired socialist transformation.

What was wrong therefore was not so much the framework of the strategy as the neglect of political economy. There was no clear identification of the political and socio-cultural conditions for effective implementation of the economic strategy. The failure therefore lay in taking a narrowly economic rather than a politico-economic and macro-sociological view of the process of socialist transformation and not formulating the political and social strategy as required. The missing element in the Indian strategy has been, therefore, the absence of mobilisation of the political, social, ethical and cultural forces needed for socialist transformation and using them for giving a socialist flavour to the economic process.

Even those sections of the elite who had adequate commitment to the socialist ideal have failed to undertake the needed social mobilisation because of certain basic weaknesses. Partly it was their unwillingness to accompany their socialist professions with socialist practice and show readiness to share poverty with the less privileged sections of society. Partly it is the absence on their part of adequate knowledge and understanding of the Indian social and cultural structure and the resistance it stimulated to a socialist society. What are the hard points of this structure obstructing socialist transformation that had to be neutralised or altered to facilitate implementation of any economic strategy for socialist transformation? Answers to these questions have not been sought in terms of Indian experience and realities but mostly in terms of what was done in other countries. The sharp division and disunity between various sections of the Left movement in India is also to be attributed partly if not wholly to this intellectual lacunae. An Indian road to socialism can be evolved only by better and keener perception of Indian conditions by the socialist groups.

The other basic weakness has been that the leadership of the socialist movement has come predominantly from upper and intermediate classes and castes and it has remained by and large concentrated in these classes and castes. Even the class composition of the leadership of those calling themselves socialist parties is an upper and middle class with their base similar to that of the mixed parties like the Indian National Congress. The westernised or, more precisely, the anglicised and predominantly urban character of the political elites in India has prevented these elites from active interaction with the Indian masses who are predominantly illiterate and rural in their social character. This gap has led to the continuing lack of education of the masses in the principles of socialism and of their activisation and organisation for defence and implementation of socialist policies. The widespread laxity and lack of social discipline among all sections of Indian society is also partly due to this lack of rapport between the elite and the masses. Similarly, the upper and middle class character of the administrators and the technocrats is also a serious impediment. They are most often apathetic if not hostile to socialist objectives. Nothing has been done to either restructure or reorient the administration to make it favourable to the process of socialist transformation, though it has been given a dominant role in implementing socialist policies. Nor was any action taken on the political plans to prevent the decline in the core of committed members in the ruling party and the increase in the number of professional and mercenary followers who came in because of electoral politics and dividends from thedevelopment process.

Earlier we identified two alternative economic patterns of a mixed economy which we called Types A and B, the first favourable to the capitalist and the second to the socialist transformation. We conclude by identifying two alternative political patterns or power structures associated with a mixed economy within a parliamentary democratic framework. One is based on a political alliance of the intermediate classes with upper classes, resorting to socialist ideology only to win mass support but using all levers of power to facilitate a type of capitalist development in the interest of narrow sections of Indian society. The other is based on the political alliance of the have-nots and the intermediate classes, using socialist ideology to release mass energy and initiative on a vast scale and using the levers of power to promote the process of socialist transformation of the economy in the interest of the widest sections of Indian society, especially of those at the bottom. The former is likely to be linked to Type A referred to earlier, while the latter is likely to be linked to Type B.

In this connection, it is of intriguing historical interest to note how Jawaharlal Nehru himself anticipated such a future, during the course of his famous Presidential Address to the Lucknow session of the Indian National Congress in 1936.

> The middle classes are a vague group of groups at the top, a handful of them are closely allied to British imperialism;

at the bottom are the dispossessed and other groups who have been progressively crushed by economic circumstances and out of whose ranks come the advanced political workers and revolutionaries; in between are the centre groups, which tend often to side with the advanced elements, but which also have alliances with the upper groups and live in the hope of joining their superior ranks. A middle class leadership is thus often a distracted leadership, looking in two directions at the same time. In times of crisis and struggle, when unity of aim and activity is essential, this two-faced leadership is bound to injure the cause and to hold back when a forward move is called for. Being too much tied up with property and the goods of this world, it is fearful of losing them, and it is easier to bring pressure on it and to exhaust its stamina . . . . . . How is this problem to be solved then? Inevitably, we must have middle class leadership but this must look more and more towards the masses and draw strength and inspiration from them. The Congress must be not only for the masses, as it claims to be, but of the masses; only then will it really be for the masses. I have a feeling that our relative weakness today is due to a certain decay of our middle elements and our divorce from the people at large. Our policies and ideas are governed far more by this middle class outlook than by a consideration of the needs of the great majority of the population. . . . . This is partly due, I think, to a certain historical growth during the last fifteen years to which we have failed to adapt ourselves, to a growing urgency of economic problems affecting the masses, and to a rising mass consciousness which does not find sufficient outlet through the Congress. This was not so in 1920 and later, when there was an organic link between the Congress and the masses, and their needs and desires, vague as they were, found expression in the Congress. But as those needs and desires have taken more definite shape, they have not been so welcome to other elements in the Congress and that organic connection has gone . . . . . The middle class claim to represent the masses had some justification in 1920; it has much less today, though the lower middle classes have still a great deal in common with the masses.

> Partly also our divorce from the people at large is due to a certain narrowness of our Congress constitution. The radical changes made in it fifteen years ago brought it in line with existing conditions then, and it drew in large numbers and became an effective instrument of national activity. Though the control and background were essentially middle class and city, it reached the remotest village and brought with it political and economic consciousness to the masses, and there was widespread discussion of national issues in city and village alike. One could feel the new life pulsating through this vast land of ours and, as we were in harmony with it, we drew strength from it. The intense repression by the government during later years broke many of our physical and outward bonds with our countryside. But something more than this happened. The vague appeal of earlier days no longer sufficed and, on the new economic issues that were forcing themselves on us, we hesitated to give a definite opinion. Worse even than the physical divorce, there was a mental divorce between the the middle class elements and the mass elements. Our constitution no longer fitted in with changing conditions; it lost its roots in the soil and became a matter of small committees functioning in the air. It still had the mighty prestige of the Congress name behind it and this carried it a long way, but it had lost the living democratic touch. It became a prey to authoritarianism and a battleground for rival cliques fighting for control, and, in doing so, stooping to the lowest and most objectionable of tactics. Idealism disappeared, and in its place there came opportunism and corruption. The constitutional structure of the Congress was unequal to facing the new situation; it could be shaken up anywhere almost by a handful of unscrupulous individuals. Only a broad democratic basis could have saved it, and this was lacking.

The economic pattern leading to socialist transformation is thus inseparable from a political and socio-cultural pattern favourable to such a transformation. From the above, the conclusion is inescapable that socialist transformation of the Indian economy has been thwarted by powerful obstructions to socialism that exist in the non-economic plane. And it is only by neutralising these non-economic obstructions that success will be achieved in both implementing and achieving socialist transformation and ensuring adequate development of the Indian economy.

REFERENCES

1. Oscar Lange, Some Problems Concerning Economic Planning in Under developed countries, (Report Writren in May 1955 in Indian Statistical Institute, Calcutta).
2. Gunnar Myrdal, *Asian Drama : An Inquiry into the Poverty of Nations*, Vol. I, Harmondsworth, Penguin Books, 1968, p. 66.
3. A striking illustration of the failure that results from neglect of socio-cultural factors even by a committed and well-intentioned Government in the field of land reforms is given by P. Radhakrishnan in his paper on 'Land Reforms in Theory and Practice—the Kerala Experience' (*Economic and Political Weekly*, Vol. 16, No. 52, Dec. 26, 1981, pp. A-129 to A-137. He points out how in actual practice, the measure resulted in transfer of ownership to rich cultivators who had leased land to supplement their holdings and created uneconomic and non-viable holdings which did not lead to self-cultivation on the part of agricultural labourers and sub-marginal cultivators but only to sale, re-sale, or leasing out to better placed cultivators. Even the Communist Government's attempt at land reform did not result in economic development with social justice on the agrarian front in Kerala, because of the neglect of socio-political and socio-cultural factors on their part and failure to institute necessary follow-up action.

8 Did India Miss the Socialist Bus?

When Gandhiji launched his mass movement for India's independence. there was no mention of our striving for a socialist society, though a socialist revolution had broken out in Russia, and more moderate and gradualist movements in a socialist direction had been operating in western countries, including the country which ruled over India. Gandhiji's primary objective was Swaraj, which meant replacement of British rule by Indian rule. But many of the elements of a socialist society were contained in the ideology with which he attempted to move the people and harness their participation in the freedom movement. The main target in his wooing were the masses. He wanted the Hindus and Muslims to forget their historical animosities and come together as Indians, whose joint interest, in social and economic terms as well as political, lay in the achievement of Indian freedom. He wanted the caste Hindus to give up their centuries-old tradition of the discrimination they had been practising against a sizeable number of their faith, calling them untouchables and denying them a place of dignity in their society. He was also appalled at the stark poverty of the bulk of his countrymen most of whom lived in the rural areas and suffered from total or partial unemployment. He wanted them to participate in the national struggle in order to get rid of their poverty, and sponsored concrete measures for giving them some immediate relief by his Khadi and Village Industries Programme. Hindu-Muslim unity, abolition of untouchability, and economic amelioration of the poor by finding them productive work formed the three planks of the programme on which he based his freedom struggle, reinforced by the sentiment of national dignity, achievable through the overthrow of foreign rule. Freedom to him meant not only political independence; it also meant the opportunity to create a just and mass-oriented new society which he called *Ram Rajya* to evoke the traditional feeling that people had that they had an ideal society during the days of Rama, whose story was public knowledge. Gandhi was of course no socialist in the accepted sense of the term. He was not a Marxist, he did not call for a democratic socialism that gave the state and governmental machinery such a powerful role in socio-economic affairs, he had a living faith in religion and in God, and he saw no distinction between ethics and economics in his ideal society nor any domination of the individual by society. All the same there can be no doubt that his movement paved the way for mass perception of the need for a fraternal, egalitarian, and just society through political freedom in place of the caste and communal ridden unequal and unjust society that was being propped up under foreign rule. The message of the New India that he carried to the masses was certainly not socialist in the accepted sense, but it was not capitalist either, and it undoubtedly sowed the seeds of a socialist climate in the country.

The educated elite whom he drew into the struggle, especially the younger among them, were largely influenced by the socialist ideas current in western teachings and the great October Revolution which appeared to have brought a socialist society into concrete being in the Soviet Union. The foremost among them was Jawaharlal Nehru, whom Gandhi treated with special affection and to whom he gave a place next only to himself in the national leadership, though neither of them made any secret of their many differences in ideological matters. Their basic identity lay in the desire for national freedom and the use of such freedom for building a just and good society. Nehru made no secret of his belief in the need for a socialist society for solving the problem of Indian poverty and, through it, the problem of social discrimination and feudal authority which were also plaguing his country. When, at the instance of Gandhi, Nehru was elected President of the Indian National Congress, though many of its leaders who were also staunch followers of Gandhi were by no means enamoured of what they thought was western-oriented socialist ideology which had no relevance to Indian conditions, they accepted the move out of a sense of loyalty to Gandhi and also the more practical consideration that Nehru enjoyed a personal position of popular admiration which could help in the harnessing of the support of the younger generation to the freedom movement. Nehru, undaunted by the feeling that he was ahead of the Congress leadership in his social and economic thinking, boldly proclaimed his faith in a socialist ideology during the course of his Presidential Address at Lucknow in 1936. After pointing out that socialism was not just an economic doctrine but a way of life, he went on:

> I see no way of ending the poverty, unemployment, the degradation and subjection of our people except through socialism. That involves vast and revolutionary changes in our political and social structure, the ending of the vested interests in land and industry, as well as the feudal and autocratic Indian states system. That means the ending of private property, except in a restricted sense, and the replacement of the present profit system by a higher ideal of cooperative services. *It means ultimately a change in our instincts, habits and desires. In short it means a new civilisation, radically different from the present capitalist order.*[1]

And he inducted three socialists into the working commitee, namely, Jaya Prakash Narain, Acharya Narendra Dev and Achyut Patwardhan, though the rest of the members were old timers who were conservative in their economic and social outlook.

Earlier, as a result of the discussions they had in the Nasik prison, a number of young Congressmen led by Jaya Prakash Narain found themselves in agreement on the socialist ideal and critical of Gandhi's thesis of trusteeship, his policy of compromise with the Viceroy, and what they considered the non-modern approach of the older men in the Congress. Nevertheless, their loyalty to the Congress was unshaken as it was the only mass organisation struggling for national freedom. They may have thought of joining the Communist Party whose ideology had brought about a comprehensive socialist change in Russia but were disgusted at that party's treatment of the nationalist movement and their calling it 'bourgeois nationalism' and Gandhi a lackey of Indian capitalists. They therefore decided to form a new party but within the Congress, as they wanted both independence and socialism, their idea being to function as a pressure group within the Congress pushing it in a socialist direction. While their activities were not relished by the older men in the Congress leadership, Gandhi characteristically gave them his indulgence and Nehru of course his wholehearted moral support. The C.S.P. or the Congress Socialist Party they formed and Nehru's avowed socialist position helped to propagate socialist ideology in the country, linking it with the national movement and the Congress hold on the masses.

The other socialist element in the country, with a similar approach to capitalism and landlordism, but differing fundamentally in its methodology and taking its cue from the Moscow-dominated Communist International, refrained from joining the national mainstream by its opposition to Gandhi and the 1930 movement; and to that extent failed to strengthen the link between socialist ideology and the mass struggle for national independence. They changed their attitude when the growing menace of Hitler led the Communist International to sponsor the idea of a United Front and, with the help of Jaya Prakash, joined the C.S.P. in large numbers and also found their way into the Congress. But their idea in joining the C.S.P. was not to strengthen the socialist pressure group within the Congress but to use their position to get more contact with the masses in both the urban and rural areas and get control over organisational positions of power. Their loyalty was extra-territorial because of the identity of their ideology with the Soviet Union; and by 1938, the C.S.P. was so disgusted that communists were thrown out of its membership. But damage had been done to the C.S.P. effort of pressurising the Congress to move in a socialist direction; and the split that took place between the leftist and moderate adherents to a socialist ideology left a trail of bitterness and mutual antagonism that certainly weakened the influence that socialist ideology was acquiring on nationalism, of which the most powerful and country wide expression was the Indian National Congress. The communists certainly gained as a separate identity, but in the process weakened the socialist pressure on the Congress and to that extent the prospects of a peaceful transition to a socialist society if and when the national struggle succeeded and the Congress came into power in independent India. The subsequent behaviour of the Communist Party, their initial opposition to the second World War in line with the Congress sentiment, their subsequent support to it with the entry of the Soviet Union, and their opposition to the national struggle and the Quit India movement, reminiscent of the anti-national position they had taken in the 1930 movement, again put them outside the mainstream of the national movement and weakened the link which was being built up between socialist ideology and the national movement.

Meanwhile the C.S.P. influence had been growing among the rank and file of the Congress and was also strengthened by the influence acquired by Subhash Chandra Bose and his leftist following. Of course, Nehru's socialist ideas also helped in the process. It was unfortunate that while Gandhi had had an excellent personal rapport with Jawaharlal Nehru, the opposite was the case with Subhash Chandra Bose. It was probably due to the fact that while Nehru differed from Gandhi in many ways, he gave him his unstinted loyalty both on personal and national grounds. Bose, on the other hand, could not stand what he thought were Gandhi's obscurantist ideas, was not sufficiently owerawed by his personality, and was prepared to challenge his leadership. He got elected to the Presidentship of the Congress despite Gandhi's opposition and presided over the Haripura Congress. His triumph was, however, shortlived. The Haripura Congress adopted Pandit Govind Vallabh Pant's resolution that Bose should consitute his Working Committee in consultation with Gandhi; and this was done with the support of Nehru. The C.S.P. members did not vote against the resolution out of loyalty to Gandhi, even though their sympathies were not with the resolution. Bose resigned and left the Congress taking with him a number of his followers. If Bose had not left the party and had made an expedient compromise with the right wing biding his time to get majority control for the left wing, the socialist position in the Congress would have been different. Also Bose may not have left the Congress if Nehru had voted against Pant's resolution or the

C.S.P. members had more actively opposed it. Anyway Bose did leave the Congress and with bitterness. The result was a further weakening of socialist pressure on Congress policy. As pointed out by Myron Weiner,

> With the exodus of the left-wing and the refusal of the socialists to leave the Congress with Bose, the socialists were left without strength either among the left wing or in the Congress Party.

The 1942 movement gave the socialists in the Congress the opportunity to recover their position. With the arrest of Gandhiji and all the senior Congress leaders and many of their orthodox following, leadership of the Quit India movement fell into the hands of the socialists and the younger members of the Congress. Their leaders went underground and J.P. became the leader and virtual hero of the Quit India movement. With his release on 12 April 1946 his new stature in the national movement became evident to all who could see or hear. By that time the Cabinet Mission had come with its proposals for a settlement, and Congress leadership appeared ready for a compromise. But J.P. was in no mood for a compromise. He wanted the Congress to launch another struggle against the British and threatened that his Congress Socialist Party would leave the Congress and do it alone if the elders in the Congress refused his request. He was certain that the British were not ready to leave, did not intend to give India freedom, and that an all-out struggle was necessary before freedom could be achieved. J.P. undertook a countrywide hurricane tour and was greeted everywhere by milling crowds shouting 'Long Live Free India. Long Live Jaya Prakash. Long Live Socialism'. He had now become the General of the Left Wing of the Congress and inheritor of the mantle left by Subhash Chandra Bose. When Nehru, as the then Congress President, invited Jaya Prakash (J.P.) to join the Working Committee and Lohia to become the General Secretary, the offer was rejected, J.P. asserting that the Constituent Assembly of the Cabinet Mission's thinking would not have any real power to make the country independent and rid it of British forces and the British financial stranglehold. Even Gandhi was not able to persuade either J.P.

or Lohia to change their decision. When the Working Committee placed a resolution before the A.I.C.C. for accepting the Cabinet Mission's proposal to form a Constituent Assembly, it was bitterly opposed by the Socialists in the party with J.P. leading the attack. He asserted:

> Congress is occupying itself in sitting in powerless parliaments passing laws when it should be out leading the masses and working for their welfare, for the abolition of untouchability and the caste system, for equality between men and women, for price control and the fixing of minimum wage for labourers. The struggle for freedom, national unity, and bread does not cease with the acceptance of the British proposals. Acceptance will let loose many forces of national disintegration.[2]

Gandhi replied and told Jaya Prakash that if there were shortcomings in the Constituent Assembly, it was for him to get them removed, and said that 'it should be a challenge to combat, not a ground for rejection'. The Working Committee's resolution was carried by 204 votes to 51; and Congress accepted the Cabinet Mission's plan to form an Interim Government at the centre prior to election for the Constituent Assembly. The Congress had not anticipated that the Muslim League would withdraw its previous acceptance of the Cabinet Mission Plan and launch on a direct struggle for the achievement of Pakistan. What Jaya Prakash had wanted the Congress to do by resuming its struggle for the achievement of freedom with the opportunity to build a socialist India, Jinnah made his Muslim League do for the achievement of Pakistan in but his own way, unleashing the forces of communal violence all over the country and using his party Government in Bengal to aid in the process. Faced with this national calamity, J.P. resumed his seat on the Congress Working Committee and threw all his weight against the communal carnage and spent himself working for communal harmony, specially in his home State of Bihar which had witnessed Hindu communal frenzy in retaliation to Muslim communal frenzy in Calcutta which had triggered off Jinnah's 'Direct Action Day', In spite of or because of the communal outbreaks, the Viceroy permitted the Muslim League to join the Interim Government, with Jinnah's views unchanged on the goal he had set for himself and his party. The fight between the Congress and the Muslim League was now carried into the corridors of power in Delhi with the Viceroy playing the role of a passive or probably partial arbitrator. The Congress gamble in accepting the Cabinet Mission proposals had not paid off. But would their acceptance of J.P's proposal have led to any better result? Could the Congress have fought—both the British and the Muslim League at the same time? Even at this distance of time, it is difficult to be dogmatic about an answer. Perhaps if J.P. had heeded Gandhi's appeal and accepted the Working Committee's resolution in the light of the political dictum that the ideal is not always the practical, or Gandhi's political wisdom of being content with one step at a time without forsaking the ultimate goal, things may have turned out differently. Jinnah may not have withdrawn his earlier acceptance of the Cabinet Mission proposals in the face of a united Congress, there may have been no direct action day, and Indian history at the dawn of independence may have been different, even if it had not been able to avoid the partition of India and the emergence of Pakistan. But all this is just speculation, and possibly futile speculation at that, unless it contains a lesson for the future for the warring politicians who are now crowding the Indian political scene. Anyway, the Congress went on with its unilateral acceptance of the Cabinet Mission proposals and held elections for the Constituent Assembly, but without a countrywider ural and urban campaign for explaining its creation which may have given it a mass base. The Constituent Assembly which held its first meeting on 9 December 1946, was a truncated body. The Muslim League member did not attend, while members of the Congress Socialist Party did not stand for election and were therefore not represented in the Constituent Assembly. What followed is part of Indian history. Lord Wavell was replaced by Lord Mountbatten, Congress agreed to the partition of India, the new India became free on the 15th August 1947, and the Constituent Assembly, elected in 1946 without the participation of the C.S.P. members in the Congress Party, started drawing up the Constitution for independent

India. Nehru now became Prime Minister of independent India but he was the only socialist in the cabinet. The C.S.P. members, to whom he had given his moral support, were not in the Government. The communists had resumed their offensive against the Congress and were attempting a revolutionary overthrow of its government. The stage did not seem well set for the creation of a socialist society in independent India.

The conservative wing of the Congress under the leadership of Vallabhbhai Patel did well by the country by liquidating the Indian states system, to whose princely inclusion in the Constituent Assembly, J.P. had taken such strong objection. And the Republic of India, which came into existence on 26 January 1950, included the people of the Indian states with their rulers functioning as constitutional heads and power transferred to the elected representatives of their peoples. In due course, they lost even this titular position, their erstwhile territories had their boundaries re-drawn and fully integrated with neighbouring erstwhile provinces of British India, and became one country without any princely relic to disturb its oneness. J.P. had evidently been wrong when he thought that the Constituent Assembly which the Congress had accepted would be able neither to engineer the withdrawal of British rule with its armed and civilian members nor liquidate the Indian princely states system. This of course is hindsight; but perhaps if J.P. had shown more confidence in the strength of the nationalist feelings of the conservative wing in the Congress, he may have joined hands with the Congress leadership in the Constituent Assembly, the transfer of power, and the framing of the Constitution with its liquidation of the Indian states system; and waited for another day to bring in the socialist society which was also a part of his nationalist dream. Again this is speculation; but it does show that in politics, one step at a time does not necessarily mean abandonment of the ultimate goal; and meanwhile socialist pressure in and on the Congress could have persisted and grown stronger for taking socialist action when the situation became ripe for doing so. But it is also possible that he may not have been allowed to play this role by the conservative leadership in the

Congress. It was also easier for them to square accounts with the socialists who had been continually sniping at their leadership when the need for securing their cooperation for securing freedom had ceased with the achievement of freedom in August 1947. As Weiner points out "Political power—and all that it implies—had fallen into the hands of the Congress party leadership, while the socialists by refusing to enter the Constituent Assembly, the interim government or the provincial governments, shared none of that power or the prestige that accompanied it." The conservative leadership had secured their position by retaining Nehru as the Prime Minister, though it was well known that they did not agree with him on many economic and social issues and that his views coincided more with the views of the C.S.P. than of the Congress without the C.S.P. Unwittingly or by deliberate choice, the C.S.P. helped them in the process of isolating Nehru from his rightful followers. By coming into conflict with the newly established Congress governments in some of the states and the unbridled attacks made on the Congress leadership by J.P. and his colleagues, they paved the way for the success of Vallabhbhai Patel's amendment to the constitution of the Congress, denying membership to individuals holding membership of "other political parties". This was clearly aimed at the C.S.P. Gandhi's healing touch was no longer there to hold together the socialist and non-socialist wings in the Congress, and Nehru was now Prime Minister and head of a Government that rested on the support of the Congress with its now dominant conservative leadership. The last annual conference of the C.S.P. was held in Nasik in April 1948, where the general sentiment was for leaving the Congress. The Socialist Party was formed with most of the erstwhile members of the C.S.P. joining it. Later it became the P.S.P. or Praja Socialist Party, with the break-away group from the Congress formed by Acharya Kripalani, the Kisan Mazdoor People's Party (K.M.P.P.), joining it. The subsequent history of the P.S.P. is well known. There were further splits, and proliferation of the socialist parties which had originated from the Congress Party. The Communist Party, after its ill-fated adventure in Telangana, also went in for parliamentary activities and was actually able to form its own government in Kerala. This party also suffered from splits and we have now a proliferation of communist parties of various hues in the country. After the death of Nehru and a three-years spell of office by Indira Gandhi as Prime Minister with the support of an undivided Congress Party, the Congress Party now had its turn at the now familiar Indian exercises of party splits. The Congress Party split in 1969 into Congress (I) and Congress (O), but with Indira Gandhi retaining the majority and the Prime Ministership. Since then, the Congress Party has had a chequered history of splits, the end of which is not yet in sight. Indira Gandhi has returned to power after a brief spell of three years out of office, when a miscellaneous collection of opposition parties calling themselves the Janata Party was in power for two years and then split with the larger of the splinter groups in power for about a year. The Janata Party has undergone more splits with one group still calling itself the Janata Party, while the Indira Congress is now in the process of becoming the Indian National Congress Party (without a suffix or a prefix) as a result not only of the decision of the Election Commission, but also as a reflection of the weakness behind the various parties calling themselves the real or original Congress. It would require more than human ingenuity to identify the 'original' Congress; but there is no doubt that the Congress led by Indira Gandhi not only commands a majority of the electorate but also of those who call themselves Congressmen. At the time of writing therefore, Indian politics is filled with the fray of a multitude of political parties, some rightist, some leftist and some whose ideology it is difficult to identify. The dominant party, and in power at the centre and most of the states, is the Congress Party led by Indira Gandhi. The Communist Party comes next, holding power in West Bengal and Tripura and heading a coalition in Kerala. A regional party holds power in Tamil Nadu, while the remaining political parties are all in the opposition, opposing each other, almost as much as they are opposing the Indira Congress. Almost a Gilbertian situation; only it was not an opera.

Our concern here is only with attempting to answer to the question whether we misssed the bus of a socialist society. In this context, attention must be drawn to the fact that with the death of Vallabhbhai Patel in 1950, Nehru had become the unquestioned leader of the Congress Party and acquired a position where he was able to implement his socialist ideas. But, to do so he needed within the party and the Government people who were also dedicated to the cause of socialist transformation; but this he was not able to get. The Congress socialists, to whom he had given his moral support and to whose ideas he felt closer than to those of the conservative majority that filled his party, had left the Congress and become an opposition party. They fought against him and the Congress Party in India's first general elections; and so did the other leftist (of different shades) parties like the K.M.P.P. and C.P. They all got beaten at the polls, leaving him with a substantial majority of seats in both the Central Parliament and in the state assemblies. The leftists, including the Socialists who had been in the C.S.P. earlier, did not fare too badly; but they could not counter the pull of the traditional hold that Congress had on the people and the charisma of Nehru. It is difficult to say how many of those who voted for the Congress Party did so because of the traditional hold of the Congress as their oldest and largest political organisation, which had the added glamour of having won independence for the country, or because of their similarity of views with the conservative wing which still dominated the Congress, or because of their sympathy with the socialist ideas with which Nehru had been associated ever since his entry into politics, or simply because of the charisma of Nehru's personality. All these factors must have had their share in ensuring the success of the Congress Party, but there is no doubt that this success did give Nehru the authority to take the country in its social and economic development along the lines he wished. He was a socialist, but his party was not; and he had to tread warily if he wanted to take the country along the socialist path. There is no doubt that he would have been immensely strengthened in his task if the erstwhile Congress socialists had responded positively to his invitation to J.P. and colleagues in 1953 to cooperate with the Congress Party both at the parliamentary and popular levels and also share his power in government. Unfortunately, this did not happen, and Nehru was left to plough a lonely socialist furrow without the mass understanding and cooperation that the socialists or other leftists could have brought him. And so we got the curious phenomenon of an attempt at a socialist transformation through a mixed economy undertaken by a man, whose official followers did not share his ideas but who were prepared to obey him in passing resolutions or enacting legeslations or setting up institutions. No attempt was made to make the party understand the implications of what he wanted or the essential conditions of its success so eloquently portrayed in his Presidential Address to the Lucknow session of the Indian National Congress, which has been quoted earlier in this chapter. Those who sincerely believed in the socialist approach and could deliver its message in terms of its being ultimately "a change in our instincts, habits and desires, in short, a new civilisation, radically different from the present capitalist order" were ranged against him and mocked at his attempts to give a socialistic slant to the Indian society and its economy. In a way, the attitude of the socialist opposition to Nehru who, in all sincerity, was attempting in his own cautious and pragmatic way to lay the foundations for a socialist transformation was more or less contained in what J.P. wrote on 10 December 1948 about Nehru's socialism :

> There is no doubt that you will hold fast to the faith that you are leading the country to socialism, but let me say without malice or rancour that in spite of your best intentions, the country is drifting in the opposite direction. You are trying to ride two horses, which may be possible in circuses but not in historical evolution. History can move only in one direction and not two at the same time. You want to go towards socialism, but you want the capitalists to help in that. You want to build socialism with the help of capitalism. You are bound to fail in that. If you want capitalism to play its role in industrialising the country, it will demand its price and if you pay the price, you will give the go-by to socialism. That is exactly what is happening today. Bold and drastic measures are necessary in the place of which we get half-hearted diluted measures.[3]

All that happened later was the use of stronger language, more of ridicule and scorn, and more of agitation and abuse on the part of the socialist opposition to Nehru than what J.P. had written in 1948. The result was only more confusion in the public mind about what was being done by Nehru to give the country a socialist pattern of society. They did not know if it was a smoke-screen behind which vested interests hid themselves, or whether it was a genuine attempt which was being thwarted by the capitalists, landlords, and other vested interests and reactionary elements, or whether it was only a well intentioned illusion that Nehru was creating not only for the country but also for himself. In the absence of socialist education for the masses and socialist understanding by the others in his party, and with the politics of elections and adult franchise unleashing the forces of money power, casteism, communalism and regionalism, and with the continuous and malicious attacks that were mounted on him by those who should have come to his help even if they did not believe in his party, India glided into a semi-socialist society on paper. This only reflected shadows but did not have substance. And inevitably, it moved on to the climax that emerged after his death, a society torn by distrust and competing slogans and conflicting politicians, eventually leading to the erosion of values, multiplicity of political parties, and the domination of a Congress which was attacked as being authoritarian, undemocratic, and resting its power on unethical practices. There was no sign of that change in the 'national instincts, habits or desires which a socialist society promised' nor a 'new civilisation radically different from the present capitalist order'.

This is the tragedy of the Indian situation. We have all the paraphernalia of a semi-socialist society; a large public sector, nationalised banking and insurance, untouchability, declared as illegal, restrictions on monopolies and larger business houses, abolition of absentee or rentier landlordism, some redistribution of land, secularism and a favoured treatment of minorities and backward and depressed classes, a national programme of meeting basic minimum needs, cheaper credit for the smaller units in agriculture and handicrafts, and a phased programme for raising above the poverty line the population below it. The Constitution itself has been amended to include the socialist goal and give priority to the directive principles of state policy, which are semi-socialist in character, over the fundamental rights which operated in favour of capitalist enterprise. But with all that, we do not have a socialist society. Inequality in income and wealth is growing, there is no large scale redistribution of land or its cooperatisation, conspicuous and vulgar consumption is on the increase, black money is creating a parallel market, bribery and corruption are increasing, unemployment is growing, illiteracy is rampant, and poverty continues to be widespread. The incongruity of this divergence of appearance from reality is a striking feature of the attempted transformation of Indian society in a socialist direction.

Why has this happened? There are several reasons and not all of them fall within the political sphere. One may state that a major reason for the failure of the Nehruvian socialist experiment was the hostility of the socialist elements in the Indian political arena to Nehru's policies and their failure to join him or at least cooperate with him in his socialist endeavour. Nehru himself could perhaps be accused of not using his unique place in Indian politics and his position as Prime Minister to enforce a dictatorial transformation of Indian society in the socialist direction. The same could also be said of Indira Gandhi, though not in the same sense as is applicable to Nehru. The villains behind the screen are the growth of vested interests attending India's planned and unplanned economic development, the emergence of a powerful middle class both in the rural and urban areas wedded to private property and profit maximisation, the general control of the newspaper media by vested interests, the lack of understanding of the implications of a socialist society by both the classes and the masses, the unashamed pursuit of individual interests at the expense of the social good, the rapid rise of political opportunism and patronage, and a wholesale erosion of moral values and ethical standards of both individual and group behaviour. It would be difficult to conceive of such a society transforming itself into a socialist pattern through existing parliamentary methods of securing control over state machinery without either provoking a civil war or leading to an apparent change that has no basis in reality. Have we missed the bus of socialist change through parliamentary democracy? One hopes not, but the hope is feeble in the face of the overwhelming reality of the non-social and anti-social values that are today enveloping the country.

This chapter must perforce end with a note of regret. It was possible in the early fifties to effect a non-violent change in a socialist direction in Indian society. The early years following Independence were still feeling the influence of the idealism, national identity, and concern for the poor released by the struggle for freedom under Gandhi's leadership. The vested interests in Indian society had not yet organised their forces nor had they grown in power or influence. Neither the capitalist nor the Kulak class had developed any real strength, while the masses were amenable—albeit passively—to any change in the social or economic sphere, that had the authority of the Gandhi-Nehru aura behind it and was visibly and conspicuously in their favour. Vested interests were like paper tigers, which could have been neutralised and made powerless with wise and vigorous action, as Vallabhbhai Patel was able to do with the apparently powerful Indian princely order. It was possible to build up an anti-capitalist and pro-socialist ethos without provoking a civil war. Communalism, casteism, linguism and regionalism were no doubt present, but they were dormant and were not receiving any disruptive encouragement from the political forces then in operation. All that was required was a combination of socialist forces with the power for introducing socialist change that Nehru possessed both as Prime Minister and as the charismatic leader of the Indian people. The conservative elements in the Congress could have been neutralised by such a combination not only because of their awe of Nehru and affection for his person but also because of their desire for retaining a place in the ruling political hierarchy. Even the communists could have been brought in, once they had agreed to work for their socialist objective through parliamentary methods and had given up their extraterritorial tutelage. Of course, only a governmental programme, even if led by Nehru and backed by a consolidation of socialist forces with the Congress Party, would not have been enough. There had to be also a nationwide programme of socialist education of the masses in the rights and obligations they would have to assume in a socialist society; and along with that an intensive education of the educated classes in the Gandhian values of simple living, ceiling on personal incomes, and practising socialism instead of merely writing or speaking about it. All this was not beyond the bounds of possibility during the early years after Independence. All that was required was a common dedication to an accepted goal, a subordination of egocentrism and factionalism to the needs of the common cause, a spirit of give and take, avoidance of fanaticism, and willingness to pursue change not merely by legislation but also by persuasion and in phased steps rather seek to bring it about in wholesale fashion without regard for individual reactions. In short, an ideological commitment to socialism and a Gandhian approach for its achievement could have made a wholesome combination for bringing about a socialist transformation in India. The other favourable factors such as the weakness of the vested interests, the national idealism and social commitment still lingering from the independence struggle, the unwillingness and inability of the conservative elements in the Congress to fight Nehru after the death of Vallabhbhai, Nehru's charismatic personality and mass appeal besides the position of power he held as Prime Minister, and the passivity of the masses which made them amenable to change from one they trusted as they had with Gandhi and now with Nehru, an educated middle class that had not yet suffered erosion in values, and a dedicated cadre of young socialist workers—all these made possible a peaceful transition to a socialist pattern through democratic means and the parliamentary process. We could possibly have caught the democratic socialist bus in the early fifties, if. . . .This would remain one of the 'ifs' of Indian history. Whether we shall be able to get a second chance to catch this bus, one does not know. The chances do not appear to be bright, however, not only because of the proliferation and confused working of political parties and the national mess they have created, but even more because of the powerful growth of a non-socialist if not also anti-socialist middle class, the even more powerful growth of the disruptive forces of casteism, communalism, linguism and regionalism, and the growing resort to force by those who have, as well as those who do not have, property or status or position or income. Impatience for economic and social change on the part of the dispossessed is meeting with tougher and more organised resistance from the vested interests; legislation and governmental intervention have lost credibility and effectiveness; and violence is beginning to replace dialogue, persuasion, and agreement by compromise. The stage seems set for a violent upheaval, but whether even that will bring us to the bus stop of socialism, let alone enable us to catch it, the future alone can tell.

REFERENCES

1. *Collected Works of Jawaharlal Nehru,* Vol. VII, Govt. of India, p. 181.
2. Allen and Wendy Scarfe, *J.P. : His Biography*, Orient Longman, 1975, p. 183.
3. Allen and Wendy Scarfe, *J.P. : His Biography*, New Delhi, Orient Longman, 1975, p. 237.

Quo Vadis? Where do we go from here? 9

> The promised land may yet be far from us and we may have to march wearily through the deserts, but who will take away from us that deathless hope which has survived the scaffold and immeasurable suffering and sorrow; who will dare to crush the spirit of India which has found rebirth again and again after so many crucifixions? *

THE LAST chapter ended on a pessimistic note but we cannot leave it at that. It is difficult to accept the conclusion that we have finally missed the bus of a democratic socialist society by the use of peaceful means. There is no reason why we should not have a second chance, if we have really learned the lessons taught by our failure to usher in a democratic socialist society when we had the chance to do so. In this concluding chapter some suggestions are mooted that may enable us to achieve the new social order that both Gandhi and Jawaharlal desired and that has been identified here with the Indian concept of democratic socialism and to do this without the violence of a civil war or external intervention.

The advantage we have is that the framework for a socialist society is already there. The new version of the Preamble to our Constitution, the Directive Principles of State Policy, the constitutional amendment that gives some of its items priority over fundamental rights, and the amendments that have qualified some of the fundamental rights for preventing their anti-social use, the nationalisation of banking and insurance, the large and growing public sector in industry, trade and transport, the programme for the satisfying of basic needs and the needs of poor and backward sections of society, the greater attention that is now paid to rural development and the needs

* Concluding words of Jawaharlal Nehru's Presidential Address to the Lucknow session of the Indian National Congress on 12 April 1936.

of marginal and small farmers and agricultural labourers and now also rural artisans, social welfare programmes for women, children, and the handicapped, low cost housing for the low income groups, consumption credit and differential rates of interest, progressive taxation of income and wealth—all these furnish the raw material for the making of a socialist society. That they have not succeeded in doing so is the result of many factors, some human, and some institutional, to the rectification of which we should now direct our attention.

A major factor that cries out for rectification is the functioning of government. Government has now become the most important determinant of what happens to the daily economic and social life of the people, with such concentration of power, patronage and influence in its hands that its presence is felt in all walks of Indian life and at all levels. It has also become obvious by now that the kind of parliamentary democracy that has been functioning in India has not produced a socialist transformation in our society nor indeed does it seem likely to be able to do so. Would a change from the parliamentary to a presidential system of democratic government, on the lines of either the American or French system be for the better? One doubts if it will. But it needs discussion in view of the wide publicity that has been given to this suggestion in the media and its sponsoring by some persons in the ruling party.

In order to consider this question of whether a change in the system of government could lead to a better achievement of desirable social and economic goals, it is necessary to take a comprehensive view of the institutions and forces that constitute governmental power.

There are four focii of governmental power, namely, the political, executive, the legislative, the administrative and the judiciary. In a parliamentary system of democracy, the first two wielders of power are intimately linked together, with the ruling and opposition parties acting as the bridge, and ultimate power resting in the elected national legislature; while in a presidential system of democracy, power is divided between the executive, the legislative and judiciary wings of government in terms of a written constitution with the resulting checks and balances contributing to the exercise of over-all Governmental power in the national and social interest and in conformity with the normative structure of society accepted by the people. We in India have had an unfortunate experience in the working of parliamentary government with our multiplicity of parties, frequency of defections from one party to another, lack of public information on the finances raised by political parties and the sources from which they are raised, huge expenditure incurred on elections to the legislatures and absence of people's participation in the selection of candidates. Added to these are the abridgements of the democratic process which have been taking place during recent years, insecurity among the bureaucracy and a growing confrontation between the executive and the judiciary. There is nothing that a presidential system as such can do to rectify the position or assure a sound democratic system of government, quite apart from the question of establishing a socialist society. A presidential form of government has also its own dangers in view of the size of the country, the diversity among the people, and the traditions it has had of monarchical rule over many centuries. What is good in it, however, is its in-built system of checks and balances which cannot be changed at the sweet will of any government which may have a majority in Parliament. The Indian system with its written constitution does provide checks and balances, but Parliament has claimed the right to amend the Constitution in any of its provisions, including the Preamble, Directive Principles, Fundamental Rights and procedures for amending the Constitution, while the judiciary has taken the view that Parliament has no power to alter the Constitution in what it considers as its 'basic' features. The parliamentary system of cabinet government and accountability to the legislature is considered as one such basic factor, whereas, under the thesis of the ultimate supremacy of Parliament, it could be legitimate to replace the parliamentary by a nresidential form of government. What we need is not a presidential system of government but a basic reform in the working of the parliamentary system of government such as will ensure the retention of democracy and implementation of a socialist transformation of Indian society.

In the light of the Indian experience, it is clear that a multi-party system is not conducive to the proper working of parliamentary democracy, whatever may be the position in other countries. At the same time a one-party system deprives the people of their political choice and may also pave the way for a dictatorship. What is needed is a two-party system. There may even be room for a three-party system, representative of the right, middle and left attitudes, or the conservative, liberal and radical positions in regard to the normative structure of society and the working of political, economic and social institutions. However, the choice between a two-party and a three-party system really rests upon the absence of a national consensus on the normative structure of society between the capitalist democracy and socialist democracy. The Indian Constitution, broadly speaking, embodies the nationally accepted normative structure in its Preamble and in the details set out in the chapters on Directive Principles, Fundamental rights, parliamentary government and the position of the judiciary. Practically all political parties have accepted, as the national goal, a democratic, secular and socialist republic and a society imbued with the principles of liberty, equality and justice. Only these are professions that lack understanding, conviction and commitment, not only on the part of the elite but also on the part of the people at large. And it is this absence of consciousness which is responsible for the failure of the Indian experiment in socialist transformation and for the breaches that are taking place in the democratic process. What is needed therefore is a kind of compulsive national education on a large scale on what the Constitution stands for and its socialist implications. This implies that points of view opposed to the constitutional normative whether held ideologically or just practised, namely, communalism, casteism, untouchability, use of religion or language or region to promote national discord and social disharmony, private armies and organised violence, unequal incomes and wealth, unlimited property and unrestricted use of property, unlimited wants, etc., will not be allowed a hearing in the same way that treason is not permitted a hearing even in peace time. However, such a programme may be objected to on the ground that it means regimentation and totalitaranism in place of democracy. A national referendum should be held with necessary and enforced ground rules for ensuring a fair and free debate between the opposing views. Let the people as a whole be given the opportunity to endorse or repudiate the normative structure of the social, political and economic life outlined in the Constitution, and, in the process get educated and acquire conviction and commitment. Once the normative structure is accepted by the people as a whole, it should become an inviolable and unchallengeable part of the social ethos, with individual dissent or deviation treated in the same way as attempts to question national integrity and sovereignty; and no political party would be allowed to question or seek to change this structure. However, this need not mean that institution of a one party system. Parties could be formed primarily on the basis of the effectiveness with which the programmes stemming from the normative structure are operated. The ruling party would be responsible for the formulation and implementation of the programmes, while the opposition party would offer a critical examination, of these programmes from the point of view of the accepted national goals, examine and evaluate implementations and offer alternative programmes that could effectively achieve the accepted goals. Elections would thus be fought on the basis of the consistency of programmes with the accepted normative structure and the efficiency of their operation. In the process the electorate would get educated in their understanding of democractic socialism and judging the pace and efficiency of its implementation. Programmes and efficiency will thus replace professions and personalities as the criteria for choosing the party to be voted to power. The increase in political maturity and vigilance this would bring about in the people would be the best safeguard for preserving both democracy and socialism in the working of government and its organs of power.

Election expenditure will have to be regulated without regard as to whether it is incurred by the party or the candidates; and the incomes and property, not only of candidates but, of all persons with incomes and property exceeding a defined limit will be filed with the competent authority and open for public inspection. While private property will be allowed in both production and consumption goods, it will be subject to defined ceilings, the enforcement of which will be the responsibility of government with the proviso that the exercise of this responsibility is subject to the scrutiny of the legislatures, the judiciary or a semi-judicial machinery, the media, scholarly research, and voluntary organisations operating in the relevant fields. Selection of candidates for election will have to be decentralised and the local population given a much larger say in their selection. It may be useful to have some variant of the American system of primaries of registered members of the two parties that would be permitted to fight the election. Each party must have cadres enrolled on the basis of their commitment, skills and experience in the working or evaluation of public institutions and willingness to give a reasonable portion of their time for the public as distinguished from their personal interest. It is also worth considering whether the primaries for selection of candidates should not be confined to the cadres, their actual election to Parliament being left to the public at large, who constitute the ultimate sovereign in a democracy. With only two parties in the fray, the contest based not on ideology or political aggrandisement but on programmes and efficiency of operation and implementation in the context of a socialist economic structure, there should be no room for the play of money power as in the elections currently held in our country. But as an abundant precaution, election expenditure should be financed from public revenues and subjected to audit, with the Election Commission given an independent status and sole responsibility for organising and conducting the elections. In fact, like the audit, election machinery should be given an independent and constitutionally guaranteed status so that elections could be really free and fair, and candidates elected would be the real representatives of the electorate. The present system of Prime Minister and Cabinet responsibility should continue, but there should be freedom for the Prime Minister to induct talent from outside the elected members of the legislature. This means that the cabinet system will have to be diluted by borrowing from the presidential system the practice followed for the choice of ministers. In case this practice is resorted to—and in any case it should only be for a minority of the Cabinet—it should be confined to technocrats or experts and their appointment endorsed by the elected legislature as in the case of the American system. Subject to their being drawn from outside the elected legislature membership, there would be no other difference between them and the other ministers, and the Cabinet would function on the basis of collective responsibility with the Prime Minister as Chairman and the de facto head of the government.

It is also important that the governmental system should operate on a federal basis with extensive decentralisation and a whole tier of local self government bodies that would ensure people's participation and strengthen democracy and social commitment at the grass-roots level. While details regarding their constitution, functions, resources, etc., will have to be worked out, what is necessary to ensure is that they do not function in a manner disruptive of the accepted normative structure but aid in its better understanding and implementation.

There is one reform that could be suggested in regard to the legislative wing of government and that is with reference to the Rajya Sabha in the Indian system. The Rajya Sabha consists of persons elected by the state legislatures plus a small nominated element representative of art, culture and other non-party and non-political elements; and it is supposed to represent the federal element in the Indian Parliament, its members voicing the views and protecting and promoting the interests of the people of their states. In actual fact, it has not functioned that way, nor with honourable exceptions, has the nominated element, especially in recent years, made an objective and independent contribution to its deliberations. By the way in which it has been functioning and the traditions it has established, the Rajya Sabha has become a fifth wheel in the coach of government, and the amount of governmental time that it expends is in no way proportionate to the effect it has on the better functioning of government or a better ventilation of the real problems of the people either of the country as a whole or its individual states. In truth, the Rajya Sabha has not served the purpose for which it was created by the Constitution and it is a moot point whether any useful purpose will be served by its retention. It certainly does not serve the purpose of "being Philip sober to Philip drunk" which was the analogy used by my Professor more than fifty years ago when he was lecturing on the justification for having two houses of the legislature for one government. All the same, one would not be in favour of abolishing the Rajya Sabha in the new set-up suggested for a democratic socialist government in India. But in supporting its retention, drastic changes in its composition and functions may be suggested. Its membership may remain at its present number; but its composition should be equally divided between representatives of state legislatures and of professional and economic organisations after providing for the present number of nominations to give representation to art, culture, philosophy and persons of eminence. The economic organisation to be given representation should cover trade unions, industry, commerce, agriculture, banking and transport, while the professional organisation to be given representation should include doctors, lawyers, scientists, social scientists, environmental specialists, regional planners, social workers, managers, teachers, bankers, co-operators and retired civil servants. Their main function would be tobring in professional and functional expertise and experience into the making of legislation and the evaluation of implementation programmes. Their function would also include the bringing in of state experience and the federal view. Their legislative and other powers may be the same as those currently exercised by the Rajya Sabha.

The third focii of governmental power, namely, the bureaucracy, amongst whom may be included government officials at all levels, from the secretaries and heads of departments at New Delhi and the state capitals to the *gram sevaks* (the village level worker) and other rural officials whose work lies in many villages of this country, the emphasis should not merely be on academic qualifications and technical skills but also on giving them social awareness and commitment to the accepted normative structure. This can be done only if there is provision for pre-service training at all levels which would give them the necessary orientation. And there should be in-service' training and workshop or seminar or *Shibir* (get-together for sessions on self-criticism) programmes at periodic intervals and at appropriate levels. Every promotion to a higher position should be preceded by a well-thought-out orientation programme of a short duration. Institutions for imparting such training and orientation programmes should be made an essential part of the governmental machinery; and the assistance of voluntary organisations, social workers and persons with a known record of social commitment and administrative or other work experience involving handling personnel and dealing with the people should also be harnessed. And every official, specialist or generalist, whose work covers a district or even a while taluka or sub-division or block should get an exposure at grass-roots level to the social and economic handicaps from which the vast majority of our people—the poor, the disinherited and the backward—suffer and the human implications and relations behind. their suffering; and this can be done only by giving them some experience of participatory functioning with the problems of the poor at the grass-roots level. At the same time, we must not forget that government service is an economic livelihood and should give them at least a nationally acceptable minimum living standards. And, while there should be an automatic adjustment (the ideal would be indexing of all governmental employees' compensation) in salaries and wages to neutralise inflationary increases in the cost of living, time-scales of pay should be supplemented by incentive payments for identifiable special efficiency, innovations or other unusual contributions by government officials to the implementation of programmes. Appropriate provision should also be made not only by executive orders but also by institutional means for receipt and disposal of public grievances, and public relations cells set up in all departments. The machinery for the operation of public enterprises should be streamlined, with decentralisation in decision making, autonomy in operations, internal promotions, and recognition of any special contribution that any enterprise may make to the general or some specific elements of the efficient functioning of the normative structure derived from the democratic socialist ideology. Worker participation in management should be an integral feature of the operation of all public sector enterprises.

The fourth unit of governmental power, namely, the judiciary has to be guaranteed its autonomy and independence by the Constitution and there should be no executive interference in its operation. The kind of inroads we have recently witnessed on the independence of the judiciary must be rectified and they should not be made the subject of popular agitation. At the same time, it should always be open to the legistature to pass necessary legislative measures to see that the normative structure embodied in the Constitution is not diluted or violated by judicial decisions. Some machinery will have to be devised for seeing that appointments to the judiciary are independent of political influence and do not become a matter of patronage in the hands of the ruling party. The three wings of government, the executive, the legislature and the judiciary should not only work in co-ordination but also act as checks and balances on the unrestrained or uncalled for use of their individual powers, always bearing in mind the supremacy of the normative structure accepted by the people and embodied in this Constitution, and the need for implementing its realisation.

Any political system that is to ensure growth, civil freedom and social justice has to have an in-built system of checks and balances on the main daily wielders of political power, namely, the political executives or ministers, the people's representatives or the legislatures, the administrative executive or the bureaucracy, and the judiciary. Operating under the restraint of these checks and balances, these wielders of governmental power should be assisted in the use of this power for the fulfilment of the nationally accepted social and economic goods (embodied in the case of India, in the Preamble to the Constitution, Directive Principles of State Policy, and the relevant articles and chapters in the Constitution) by the wielders of non-governmental power in the community, namely,v oluntary organisations of people committed to common objectives for their members, namely the business community, the trade unions of industrial, agricultural and other categories of workers, organisations of peasants and farmers, professional organisations, youth organisations and social, cultural and religious organisations. Exercising influence rather than power, and, at least ideally, committed to the overall social and economic national interest and displaying objectivity in their perception of the different wielders of power are what is known as the Fifth Estate or the media and information systems, and the intellectuals, thinkers and writers who take interest in public affairs. It is the social commitment, behavioural pattern, knowledge, efficiency and way of life of these focii of power and influence, that would determine government's ability to usher in a democratic socialist society rather than its form as a presidential or a parliamentary system of democracy. Behind all these forces is the ultimate sovereign in the democratic system, namely, the people. It is the people's social and political awareness and their emotional commitment to the twin concepts of individual human worth and economic growth with social justice that will determine their ability to exercise their sovereignty. Only then can they ensure that the system of government and its checks and balances does not result in misuse of power or failure or tardiness in bringing about the desired socialist transformation of the Indian hue that has been discussed in earlier chapters of this volume.

The ultimate sovereign in the democratic system are the people of the country. They must have positive feeling of national identity, religious harmony and secular mutuality, equality of human dignity and individual worth, a rational outlook and a scientific temper, pride in self-reliance, a cooperative spirit and commitment to the work ethic, production efficiency and economic growth with social justice, ecological and population balance and environmental health. Such a state of the people can neither be taken for granted nor can it be achieved without purposive and deliberate action taken for the purpose. We in India have many inherited and traditional handicaps to overcome to reach this stage. Superstition, rituals, taboos, unsocial and anti-social customs, discriminatory treatment of women, caste ties, fatalism and communal animosities, all falsely attributed to religious sanction, and failure to practise the ethical and human heritage of our historical religions are all a part of the Indian cultural ethos which stand in the way of economic growth, social cohesion, emotional identity and a socialist transformation.

In this connection, a pertinent extract from an article in the *Indian Express* of 22 June 1981 by Acharya J.B. Kripalani* the nonagenarian veteran student of Indian public affairs :

> In India that is Bharat, Socialism is consistent with the caste system and untouchability: palaces stand side by

*The Acharya has since passed away.

side with slums; socialism can accommodate big industries in the private sector making huge profits, even exist check by jowl with the egregious black market. Then there is the most modern textile industry which coexists with *takli*, *charka*, handloom and other village and and cottage industries. All these constitute Indian socialism. There is no incongruity at all.

The ancient Indians believed in forecasts made by priests and astrologers. This custom remains intact even among those who pride themselves as votaries of science and parade their rationalism. Like every prince in the past, almost every Minister in India has an astrologer. He is consulted on all important occasions, in getting ministerships, jockeying for higher positions, in the Government and success in business.

These few examples help to drive home the point that in India, the new does not replace the old; it is tradition in modernity. Has not Kalidasa said, "The old is not all pure, nor the new all corrupt. And who can find fault with us for making one complement the other?"

Acharya Kripalani is known for his devastating wit and sarcasm. There is a great deal of uncomfortable truth in what he writes. But he does not suggest that we should destroy all that is old and replace it only by what is new. The essential truth behind his remark is his quotation from Kalidasa. What we need in our cultural ethos is the combining or fusion of the pure in the old and the non-corrupt in the new; and this is also what underlies what one can call the Indian approach to socialism.

There is much in our composite cultural heritage that can help in our social and ethical advancement, economic development, national integration and socialist transformation. There is also much in our cultural and social heritage that is hindering the attainment of these objectives. Poverty and illiteracy contribute to the obstructive process and so also the inadequacy and irrelevance of our educational system. We need a lot of spring cleaning, and clearing up of cobwebs, dirt and disorder in our cultural and social heritage. What we need is—and the phrase is used even at the risk of being misunderstood since no other phrase can adequately connote the process that is pictured in one's mind —a thorough and effective cultural revolution and rejuvenation. This permeation has to instil in the hearts and minds of our people the basic values of democratic socialism that have been referred to so frequently in earlier pages. Equality—social, political and economic, human dignity and individual worth, civil freedoms and the link between rights and duties, communal harmony and mutual respect for all religions, people's participation and local self-government, national and social discipline, the dependence of professions for their credibility on practice, work ethic, self respect and self reliance, economic growth with social justice, self-criticism and social accountability, the location of ultimate power and sovereignty in the people, and the superiority of social and ethical values over individual ambitions and self-aggrandisement—all these constitute both the path and the goal, the means and ends, of a democratic socialist transformation. In fact this is the normative structure that our society requires; and it is an understanding of what it means, an absorption of its content as an intellectual and emotional conviction, and an acceptance of the individual and social obligations it imposes and the privileges it confers that should be the objective of the suggested permeation.

This grand idea for a national cultural revolution should not be dismissed either as an utopian fantasia or a benighted and malignant exercise in regimentation. What is advocated is the daily reiteration of the values we stand for and condemnation of the departures from their practice; and these are the values that are embodied in our Constitution, are distilled from our spiritual heritage, and are supported in the sayings and doings of all great men of vision and wisdom who have strode through human history, including our Gandhiji of blessed memory, who not only fought for India's political freedom but also strove for the rediscovery and recovery of her soul. No one can dispute the supreme power of consciousness to determine human behaviour patterns, though the carrot and the stick are the most frequently used instruments for this purpose in human history. One cannot dispute either the relevance or the comparative efficacy of the carrot-stick approach that has been used not only in capitalist societies and now in socialist societies but even in religious preachings which promise rewards for conformity and punishments for deviance. But it cannot be disputed either that consciousness of right and wrong can be a great help in making the carrot-stick system work and, in fact, make the system itself unnecessary if the consciousness is complete. Propaganda is an ugly word, especially when it is aimed at the mind and the heart; but this has not made us desist from using it either for selling goods and services or destroying the other fellow's or group's or nation's property or killing people for impersonal reasons. We also use it for good causes like concern for the blind, the deaf, the handicapped, spastic children, the mentally retarded etc., or for more mundane causes like traffic sense, hygiene, avoidance of environmental pollution or degradation, ecological balance or population control and family welfare. The good word is education; and attempts at creating consciousness become education when they are used for propagating the right values, while it becomes propaganda when used for propagating the wrong values and gets rightly condemned as 'brain-washing'. The cultural revolution suggested here to make socialist democracy work in India is for the propagation of the right values, values that we accepted as right in the past and accept as right in the present and indeed the world as a whole has accepted. Only, and it is almost a fatal handicap, we have not practised what we accepted. We have mixed up the right values with many that are wrong but given them a semblance of consistency by the distorted use of our minds and imagination. When we do lay emphasis on the right values, we seek their implementation in selective and partial fields, denying their wholeness to a good life, and use the stick-carrot approach as sanctions for the implementation. We have sadly neglected the role of education in creating consciousness of right values in the pupils. We have confined education either to rote or skills or the sharpening of the mind and sometimes of the imagination but failed to use it to stimulate the consciousness of human identity and all the right values that flow from such recognition. The ethical values that flow from the Indian concept of Vedanta would be an ideal base for creating the consciousness that can make a socialist society viable; but Vendanta is meant for philosophers